Proceedings of the

19th International Congress of Classical Archaeology

Volume 7: The Economic Structure of Eastern Anatolian Highland from Urartian Period to the End of Late Antiquity

Proceedings of the 19th International Congress of Classical Archaeology

Cologne/Bonn, 22 – 26 May 2018

Archaeology and Economy in the Ancient World

Edited by

Martin Bentz and Michael Heinzelmann

Volume 7

ICCA
XIX
AIAC

Edited by

Mehmet Işikli

The Economic Structure of Eastern Anatolian Highland from Urartian Period to the End of Late Antiquity

Panel 2.6

Propylaeum
SPECIALIZED INFORMATION
SERVICE CLASSICS

Bibliographic information published by the Deutsche Nationalbibliothek:
The Deutsche Nationalbibliothek lists this publication in the Deutsche Nationalbibliografie;
detailed bibliographic data are available on the Internet at http://dnb.dnb.de.

Propylaeum
SPECIALIZED INFORMATION SERVICE CLASSICS

Published at Propylaeum,
Heidelberg University Library 2022.

This publication is freely available under https://www.propylaeum.de (Open Access).
URN: urn:nbn:de:bsz:16-propylaeum-ebook-707-1
DOI: https://doi.org/10.11588/propylaeum.707

Editorial Coordination: Florian Birkner, Ina Borkenstein, Christian Schöne
Editorial Staff: Stefanie Herten, Katharina Zerzeropulos

Layout: Torsten Zimmer, Zwiebelfisch@quarium

Cover illustration: The Western Storage rooms of Ayanis Castle.
Photo: Ayanis Castle Excavation Archive.

ISBN: 978-3-948465-74-2
e-ISBN: 978-3-948465-73-5

Universität zu Köln
UNIVERSITÄT BONN

CONTENTS

PREFACE

On behalf of the 'Associazione Internazionale di Archeologia Classica (AIAC)' the 19th International Congress for Classical Archaeology took place in Cologne and Bonn from 22 to 26 May 2018. It was jointly organized by the two Archaeological Institutes of the Universities of Cologne and Bonn, and the primary theme of the congress was 'Archaeology and Economy in the Ancient World'. In fact, economic aspects permeate all areas of public and private life in ancient societies, whether in urban development, religion, art, housing, or in death.

Research on ancient economies has long played a significant role in ancient history. Increasingly in the last decades, awareness has grown in archaeology that the material culture of ancient societies offers excellent opportunities for studying the structure, performance, and dynamics of ancient economic systems and economic processes. Therefore, the main objective of this congress was to understand economy as a central element of classical societies and to analyze its interaction with ecological, political, social, religious, and cultural factors. The theme of the congress was addressed to all disciplines that deal with the Greco-Roman civilization and their neighbouring cultures from the Aegean Bronze Age to the end of Late Antiquity.

The participation of more than 1.200 scholars from more than 40 countries demonstrates the great response to the topic of the congress. Altogether, more than 900 papers in 128 panels were presented, as were more than 110 posters. The publication of the congress is in two stages: larger panels are initially presented as independent volumes, such as this publication. Finally, at the end of the editing process, all contributions will be published in a joint conference volume.

We would like to take this opportunity to thank all participants and helpers of the congress who made it such a great success. Its realization would not have been possible without the generous support of many institutions, whom we would like to thank once again: the Universities of Bonn and Cologne, the Archaeological Society of Cologne, the Archaeology Foundation of Cologne, the Gerda Henkel Foundation, the Fritz Thyssen Foundation, the Sal. Oppenheim Foundation, the German Research Foundation (DFG), the German Academic Exchange Service (DAAD), the Romano-Germanic Museum Cologne and the LVR-LandesMuseum Bonn. Finally, our thanks go to all colleagues and panel organizers who were involved in the editing and printing process.

Bonn/Cologne, in August 2019

Martin Bentz & Michael Heinzelmann

Socio-economic Structure of the Highlands of Eastern Anatolia Region before Urartian Kingdom

Ayşegül Akin Aras

Introduction*

The region of Eastern Anatolia, located at the crossroads of cultural regions such as the Near East, the Caucasus and Iran. It is bordered by the Kura depression in the northeast, with the Urmiye Plateau in the east, with the line drawn by the Euphrates in the west and the area up to the Taurus Mountains in the south. Undoubtedly, the highland East Anatolian geography, which consists of mountain ranges reaching up to 3000 meters in height and plain areas, is one of the most difficult regions of Anatolia, both geographically and ecologically. However, the ecological niches that we encounter in the topography of the region constitute the suitable living environment for settled life. Moreover, the Eastern Anatolia region has a specific location in the sense that the region is always in interaction and communication with these cultural zones through the rivers of Kura, Araxes, Euphrates and Tigris, which rise from its of soil.

In this geography, in which high and rough mountains and continental climate have been shown, agriculture has been capable of meeting only the vital need. On the other hand, the extensive and wide grasslands and meadows help to improve livestock breeding. It is possible that the "Culture of Nomads", which was historically dominant in the Eastern Anatolia region, could be the result of such a geographic obligation.

Although animal husbandry was an indispensable life form and economic model for this geography, the fact remains that it was not the only livelihood, as the region has rich obsidian and mineral resources. Undoubtedly, these conditions had been decisive in the survival of people in this difficult geography. They used the surplus of these raw material resources as reserved product and provided interregional transfer via rivers.

One of the most important factors in the development of people's way of life, culture and economies is geography. At this point, this natural progress did not work differently in the highlands of the East Anatolian Plateau as well and the people had adapted to this harsh geography and these lands had hosted many idiosyncratic cultures. The archaeological processes for these cultures in the region have been partially revealed. In this case, the reasons such as the difficulty of the region, the insufficient research attempts and, most importantly, the lack of written tradition in the pre-Urartu period have been causing slow progress. We will try to evaluate the archaeological history and also the economic structure of the region with the limited archaeological data.

An Overview of the Socio-Economic Structure of the Region during the Prehistoric Period

When we look into the geography of the region in general, we encounter some downsides about prehistoric periods. The limited number of archaeological investigations carried out in the region is unfortunately not sufficient to illuminate this period.[1] Especially, in the highlands of Eastern Anatolia, which are situated in the northern part of Eastern Anatolia, this situation seems more serious, while the southern plains offer more information. The salvage excavations carried out in 1960s for the dam construction had tremendeous effects. The data from the area of the plains will help us clarify the prehistory of the highlands area.

When we have a look at the Paleolithic period of the region, a bleak picture awaits us in correlation with the scarcity of the research. However, the existence of prehistoric settlements that share mutual cultural characteristics with the neighboring southern Caucasia, reveals the potential of Eastern Anatolia. It is considered that the people with African roots in Georgia-Dmanisi.[2] performed their movement of migration from Africa to Dmanisi through Eastern Anatolia. Because of its natural territory, the habitable climatic conditions and most importantly, rich raw material resources are enough reasons for the inhabitants of the Paleolithic period to migrate here, even for a short period of time. Although the lithics (stone tools) from the Paleolithic age obtained from the regions of Erzurum, Kars,[3] Tunceli, Elazığ and Van prove the existence of settlement in the period within the region, it is not possible to talk about the economy of the region based on the few individual tools from this period. However, when we look to the south of Eastern Anatolia, it gives us data of the communities that provided their livelihood through hunting and gathering, and it is valuable data, since it indicates the possibility of similar communities living in the highlands region. It is exciting to note that the stone tools and product wastes found at the Gürgürbaba Hill (Van), which have been discovered as a result of the surveys in recent years, demonstrated that this was the living area of the Lower and Middle Paleolithic people, and that the tool production techniques and the way of life did not change.[4] The excavations that will continue in Gürgürbaba Hill in the coming years are certain to shed light on the prehistory of the highlands area. The data we have is mostly concentrated in the southern part of the region. Nonetheless, rock paintings, which has been a question at issue, are noteworthy for the highlands region.

Unfortunately, the archaeological data in Eastern Anatolia during the Neolithic period is very weak. In the excavations conducted during early periods, the rock paintings were found in Yazılıkaya, Kurbanağa Caves (Kars),[5] Gevaruk and Tırşin Highlands[6] (Van-Hakkari). As a result of stylistic evaluations on the dating of these rock paintings, many opinions were raised and the Neolithic period was the most widely accepted. However, these evaluations have never been based on analyses that will enable us to have clear information on the rock paintings.[7] The systematic research on these rock paintings, which are considered the way people express themselves, will enable us to have an idea about the history of these communities and their lives. As a matter of fact, the animal figures depicted in the rock paintings of the highlands region show the fauna of the region and their developing economies. These artefacts unearthed in the high parts of the highlands of East Anatolia lead us to the concept of the "*mountain neolithic*". Strong Neolithic traces seen in the neighboring regions Georgia and Armenia support this claim.[8] How did it all progress in Eastern Anatolia in the Neolithic Age when the foundations of the settled life were established? This is a matter of fact. Therefore, it is assumed just as an offer that the hunter and gatherer aceramic tribes living in southeastern Anatolia went to the north following the droves. It is also thought that tribes in search of raw materials and livestock, have arrived in this region and shaped its economy accordingly. At this point, the most important determining factor in the economic base of the region is the raw material relationship network based on obsidian. Thanks to its obsidian dominant raw material potential, the eastern Anatolia Region has attracted the attention of the prehistoric humankind and these resources have been utilized. Thus, as a result of the studies conducted, it is observed that the Neolithic settlements of both Caucasia and the Near East supply their raw material needs from Eastern Anatolia.

Southern Caucasus Centred Agriculture and Livestockbreeding Communities

Having a look at the Chalcolithic period of the region, it is identified that the obsidian-based trade continues also in the periods of Halaf and Obeyd. The ceramics belonging to the Mesopotamian cultures are also observed the other regions of Eastern Anatolia, particularly in Tilkitepe. Also, foundlings of obsidian and mine in the settlements of the culture exist. All of these are important in revealing the commercial relations and connections with southern cultures. The reality that Tilkitepe is located quite close to the obsidian resources and the obsidian kernels and tools obtained from the settlement, strengthen the perception that this region was an obsidian distribution center and commercial hub.[9]

In this period, one of the most important and distinctive details is that the two worlds divided into the north and south in this region becomes much more evident starting with the Chalcolithic period. While the south of the Taurus Mountains gets integrated with Mesopotamia, the northern side is more local and it is more interactive with southern Caucasia. In the south, it is possible to mention the existence of a regular economic system and specialized animal husbandry, especially in the Arslantepe settlement, where the foundations of political centralization were laid, and on the other hand the economic model of independent and pastoral lifestyle in the mountainous region was remarkable.

The recent studies show that the earliest settlement period in the highlands of Eastern Anatolia starts at the beginning of the Chalcolithic Ages.[10] In the studies carried out in limited time, unfortunately, sufficient data has not been able to provided on the cultural and economic structures of the region. It is observed that the communities in this region have a cultural and economic structure following the Neolithic and that they are made up the local tribes based on peasantry, agriculture and livestock breeding. It is seen that there is ovine breeding just like the Late Neolithic period as well as there is cattle breeding towards the ends of Early Chalcolithic period. The most eligible data about the region are the Sos Höyük excavations.[11] Sos Höyük VA layer (the late-Chalcolithic phase) revealed the existence of a simple village with a strong architectural tradition and city walls, and culture based on agriculturally supported animal husbandry and mixed food economy in the region.[12]

Kura-Araxes Peoples and Emergence of Pastoral Groups

At the Upper Euphrates Basin, where the Uruk system integrated with Mesopotamia, Arslantepe reveals that it has a progressed economic system.[13] Yet, due to an unknown reason, this system collapses and a crisis arises towards the end of the 4th millenium. The pastoral groups in crisis coming from the north caused the rise of a new culture. This new rising culture appearing in the Kura- Araxes Basin, locally known as Kura-Araxes Culture, spreads across all of Eastern Anatolia.[14]

With the beginning of Early Bronze Age, the traces of this culture, which manifested itself in a large part of the Eastern Anatolia, demonstrated itself in a wide geography from the Caucasus to the coasts of the Levant, the the Caspian coast to the Central Anatolian Plains. It is known that these communities that had settled or semi-nomadic lives in northeast Anatolia and Lake Van Basin lived on the agriculturally supported livestockbreeding.[15] This way of life, which is very similar to today's plateau model, also shows in materials very specific to the culture. One of the most important of these materials are portable hobs, which had been common in Kura-Araxes and nomadic culture.[16]

In this period of change, a complex socio-economic structure emerges in many fields such as agriculture, ceramic production, etc. The tools such as bronze and stone sickles, flint microliths and grinding stones are evidence that these groups were engaged in agricultural activities. The variety of agricultural products is not dissimilar from the Chalcolithic Age and the amount of the production varies. The puddled clay silo obtained from Van-Dilkaya Mound show that though small-scale, the storage of the agricultural products is systemized.[17]

In the Kura-Araxes Culture, it is observed that the main economic model was specialized livestock breeding, the sheep and the goat breeding continued in the Early Bronze Age as in almost every period. However, in Sos Mound settlement, which is located in the mountainous area, it was revealed that secondary production in animal husbandry remained a secondary importance.[18] Additionaly, the tools such as awl, auger, needle, spindle, spool and textile parts made by using animal bones and horns show that weaving/textile were also carried out.[19]

Data on the fact that the mining was another important economic model for this highlands geography with the agriculture-supported animal husbandry has been provided from the settlements in this period. According to the evidence of the metallurgical activities and the metal work inventory of the early excavations of Karaz, Pulur and Güzelova, and the recent finds from Sos Mound, the region had close relations with the Caucasus during the Early Bronze Age.[20]

Kurgan Peoples

Towards the end of the Kura-Araxes culture, through the migrations from the north, dynamism arose within the region. Thanks to the people coming from northern Caucasia, the region gets introduced to a new culture. The most remarkable cultural remains from these communities, whose traces can be found especially in the southern Caucasus, northwestern Iran and in some parts of the Eastern Anatolian plateau, are cairn-like tombs, high quality painted ceramics and rich metal finds unearthed from these tombs.[21] Known as the "Kurgan peoples", through these nomadic communities, life in mounds was over. The reason for the lack of data on settlements is that the communities of this era were pastoral groups and embraced the full nomadic way of life.[22] Under the light of this information, it is observed that the socio-economic structure of these communities, which are known as the first elites of the highland, an economic model based totally on stock farming developed.

Period of Beyliks

These transhumant nomadic people, later form tribes and principalities socio-politically based on kindredship. We know these principalities, which were present in the Late Bronze- Early Iron age, through their monumental castles and graveyards. It is seen that this system had a substructure that would shape the Urartu economy. There is data that animal husbandry and small-scale agricultural activities constituted the primary economic model. The grain silos gathered from the Karagündüz excavations have evidential value.[23] The changes in socio-political structure were reflected in the economic structure.[24] It is infered that control of livestock and pastures was provided by the fortresses built on the plateaus. Above all, it would not be wrong to say that the livestock economy is shaped and organized in a way that it bears no similarity with the previous periods of Eastern Anatolia, if the Late Bronze-Early Iron Age castles is considered.

It is thought that the diverse mining potential and production had an impact on the chiefdoms in the Early Iron Age in Eastern Anatolia to construct fortresses and join together to become the most important power and state structure of the Near East under the name of Urartu Kingdom. Evidence of this situation are hundreds of items, weapons and ornaments made of iron found in the cemetery areas of Ernis, Evditepe, Karagündüz, Hakkari, Şorik and Yoncatepe. In particular, the number of finds and content of them are very rare in the areas of Transcaucasia and northwestern Iran, and the development of iron metallurgy spread from Van region to neighboring regions.[25]

Conclusion

It is very difficult to talk about the economic structure of the cultures in the archaeological history of the highlands of the East Anatolia Region before the Urartu Kingdom. The lack of research due to the hard conditions in this area and especially, the fact that acquisition of written tradition only occured with the Urartus, are the challenges we are facing.

Unfortunately, the fateful destiny of the Eastern Anatolian geography is that the unchanging primary economic subsistence source is livestock. It is seen that specialization in animal husbandry has only been realized in time when the economy based on livestock supported agriculture has not changed in the historical process. Another determinant factor in the economic basis of the region is the raw material network. It is obvious that the people of the highlands of East Anatolia developed an economic system based on these two elements in almost every period.

In Eastern Anatolia during the migration of people to the Caucasus, animal husbandry and the resources of the region played a leading role for the settlements. Due to the obsidian potential of the region, it became a destination center during the Bronze Ages and provided raw materials via rivers and connection roads.

After the emerging of the Chalcolithic period in the region, the mineral deposits came into the commericial scene as another source of raw material. The transfers carried out from rich mine deposits to Mesopotamia and the data on metallurgical activities obtained from the settlements emphasize the importance of mining in Eastern Anatolia economics.

After the Chalcolithic Age, the region hosted many culturally different communities throughout the Bronze Age, but it transformed without changing its socio-economic structure. With the socio-political changes experienced in the Late Bronze-Early Iron Age, the economy of the mountainous Eastern Anatolia was coordinated and most importantly, this process formed the foundations of the Urartian economy.

Notes

* This subject has been discussed more comprehensively in Turkish in a book titled "Economic and Agricultural Life in the Ancient Ages of the Anatolia" Gökçek – Yildirim – Pekşen 2018, 459–544.

[1] Kökten 1947, 223–236; Koşay 1972, 128.

[2] Gabuni et al. 2001, 158–170.

[3] Kökten 1944, 659; Şenyürek 1944, 351; Goetze 1957, 15; Kökten 1985, 428.

[4] Baykara et al. 2016, 539–552; Baykara et al. 2017, 295–314; Baykara et al. 2018, 27–41.

[5] Kökten 1944.

[6] Özdoğan 2004, 28 f.

[7] Tümer 2017, 163–173.

[8] Badalyan et al. 2010, 185–218; Lyonette-Guliyev 2010, 219–228.

[9] Sağlamtimur 2001, 15. However, many researchers have opposed the idea of Tilkitepe's network of obsidian-oriented relationships with southern cultures. It is noteworthy that such a small-scale settlement within a 3-hour distance cannot be the center of such a commercial network. Tekin 2017, 343 f.

[10] Erkmen-Altunkaynak 2017, 237–262.

[11] Işıklı 2011, 230–233.

[12] Sagona-Sagona 2000, 55–127.

[13] Frangipane 2009, 24–41.

[14] Işıklı 2011.

[15] Piro 2009; Işıklı 2012, 103–112.

[16] Işıklı 2011, 76 f.

[17] Çilingiroğlu 1993, 471.

[18] Palumbi 2010, 158–160.

[19] Frangipane et al. 2009, 16–22; Arslantaş 2013, 382–392.

[20] Sagona-Sagona 2000, 64, fig. 48. 49; Işıklı 2008, 55–79.

[21] Miron-Orthmann 1995, fig. 67. 68. 72. The tradition of ceramic products in the region, the settlement plans and the innovations in the burial customs are related to the changing socio-economic and political structure. The rich metal finds recovered from the Cairns and these Cairns give us a picture of an elite ruling class and a newly beginning social hierarchical structure. Therefore, these communities were called „the first elites of the highlands". Işıklı 2018, 78.

[22] Özfırat 2001, 108–116.

[23] Sevin et al. 2000, 850.

[24] Belli-Konyar, 2003, 92; Erdem 2011, 59–68.

[25] Belli-Konyar 2003, 91.

References

Arslantaş 2013

Y. Arslantaş, Tarih Öncesi Dönemde Harput ve Çevresinde Tarım ve Hayvancılık Fırat Üniversitesi Harput Uygulama ve Araştırma Merkezi Geçmişten Geleceğe Harput Semzpoyumu 23–25 Mayıs 2013 Bildiri Kitabı (Elazığ 2013) 367–392.

Badalyan et al. 2003

R. S. Badalyan – A. T. Smith – P. S. Avetisyan, The Emergence of Sociopolitical Complexity in Southern Caucasia: An Interim Report on the Research of Project ArAGATS, Archaeology in the Borderlands: Investigations in Caucasia and Beyond, in: A. T. Smith – K. S. Rubinson 2003, Archealogy In The Borderlands. Investigations in Caucasia and Beyond (Los Angeles 2003) 144–166.

Baykara et al. 2016

İ. Baykara – B. Dinçer – S. Şahin – E. Koç – D. Baykara – İ. Özer – M. Sağır, 2014 Yılı Van İli Neojen ve Pleistosen Dönemleri Yüzey Araştırması, Araştırma Sonuçları Toplantısı 33 (Erzurum 2016) 539–552.

Baykara et al. 2017

İ. Baykara – B. Dinçer – S. Şahin – E. Koç – D. Baykara – İ.H. Bolkan, 2015 Yılı Van İli Pleistosen Dönem Yüzey Araştırması, Araştırması Sonuçları Toplantısı 34 (Edirne 2017) 295–314.

Baykara et al. 2018

İ. Baykara – B. Dinçer – S. Şahin – E. Koç – E. Ünal – R. Kuvanç – B. Gülseven – Ö. Birol, Van İli Neojen ve Pleistosen Dönemleri Yüzey Araştırması-2016", Araştırması Sonuçları Toplantısı 35 (Ankara 2018) 27–41.

Belli – Konyar 2003

O. Belli – E. Konyar, Doğu Anadolu Bölgesi'nde Erken Demir Çağı Kale ve Nekropolleri, Arkeoloji ve Sanat Yayınları (İstanbul 2003).

Çilingiroğlu 1993

A. Çilingiroğlu, Van-Dilkaya Höyüğü Kazıları Kapanış, 14. Kazı Sonuçları Toplantısı 1 (Ankara 1993) 469–492.

Erdem 2011

A. Erdem, Doğu Anadolu'nun Demir Çağ Aşiretleri, Tüba-Ar 14, 2011, 59–68.

Erkmen – Altunkaynak 2017

M. Erkmen – G. Altunkaynak, 2016 yılı Alaybeyi Höyük Kazıları, Müze Kurtarma Kazıları Sempozyumu (19–20 Nisan 2017) Bildiri Kitabı (Hatay 2017) 237–262.

Frangipane et al. 2009

M. Frangipane – E. A. Strand – R. Laurito – S. Möller-Wiering – M. L. Nosch – A. Rast-Eicher – A. W. Lassen, Arslantepe, Malatya (Turkey): Textiles, Tools and Imprints of Fabrics from the 4th to the 2nd Millenium BCE, Paleorient 35, 2009, 5–29.

Gabuni 2001

L. Gabuni, Dmanisi and Dispersal, Evolutionary Antropology 10, 2001, 158–170.

Goetze 1957

A. Goetze, Kleinasien, Kulturgeschichte des Alten Orients (Munich 1957).

Işıklı 2008
M. Işıklı, Erzurum'un İlk Madencileri, Atatürk Üniversitesi Güzel Sanatlar Enstitü Dergisi 21, 2008, 55–79.
Işıklı 2011
M. Işıklı, Doğu Anadolu Kura-Aras Kültürü, Arkeoloji ve Sanat Yayınları (İstanbul 2011).
Işıklı 2012
M. Işıklı, The Subsistence Economy of Kura-Araxian Folks in Eastern Anatolia: Animal Husbandary and Pastoralism", Azerbaycanın Erken Ekinçilik Dövrü Abideleri Sempozyumu (Maqalaler Toplusu), Azerbaycan Milli İlimler Akademiası Arxeologiya ve Etnoqrafiya İnstitutu (Bakü 2012) 103–112.
Işıklı 2018
M. Işıklı, Dağlık Doğu Anadolu Yaylasının Erken Halkları, Aktüel Arkeoloji 64, 2018, 72–79.
Koşay 1972
H.Z. Koşay, Pulur (Sakyol) Kazısı, 1970, ODTÜ Keban Projesi 1970 Çalışmaları, (Ankara 1972) 127–138.
Kökten 1944
İ.K. Kökten, Orta, Doğu ve Kuzey Anadolu'da Yapılan Tarih Öncesi Araştırmalar, Belleten 8/32 (Ankara 1944) 659–689.
Kökten 1947
İ.K. Kökten, Bazı Prehistorik İstasyonlar Hakkında Yeni Gözlemler, DTCFD 2/5 (Ankara 1947) 223–236.
Lyonnet et. al. 2010
B. Lyonnet – F. Guliyev, Recent Discoveries on the Neolithic and Chalcolithic of Western Azerbaijan, TUBA-AR 13, 2010, 219–222.
Miron – Orthmann 1995
A. Miron – W. Orthmann, Unterwegs zum Goldenen Vlies: Archaologische Funde aus Georgien (Saarbrücken 1995).
Özdoğan 2004
M. Özdoğan, The Neolitic and The Highlands of Eastern Anatolia, Ancient Near Eastern Studies A View From The Highlands Archealogical Studies in Honour of Charles Burney, in: Antonio Sagona (eds.), Peeters (Belgium 2004) 28–29.
Özfırat 2001
A. Özfırat, Doğu Anadolu Yayla Kültürleri, Arkeoloji ve Sanat Yayınları (İstanbul 2001).
Palumbi 2008
G. Palumbi, Red and Black Social vs. Cultural Interaction between the Upper Euphrates and Southern Caucasus Communities in the Fourth and Third Millennium BC (Rome 2008).
Sagona – Sagona 2000
A. Sagona – C. Sagona, Excavations at Sos Höyük 1998–2000 Fifth Preliminary Report, Ancient Near Eastern Studies 37 (Belgium 2000) 55–127.
Sağlamtimur 2001
A. H. Sağlamtimur, Urartu Krallığı'nın Ekonomik Yapısı (Ege Üniversitesi Sosyal Bilimler Enstitüsü Arkeoloji Anabilim Dalı Yayınlanmamış Doktora Tezi, İzmir 2001).

Sevin et al. 2000
V. Sevin – A. Özfırat – E. Kavaklı Van-Karagündüz Höyüğü Kazıları (1997 Yılı Çalışmaları), Belleten 63/238 (Ankara 2000) 847–867.

Şenyürek 1944
M. Şenyürek, Tebliğler: Anadolu'da Bulunan İki Yeni Alete Dair Bir Not, Dil Tarih Coğrafya Fakülte Dergisi 2/2 (Ankara 1944) 345–352.

Tekin 2017
H. Tekin, Tarihöncesinde Mezopotamya Yeni Yaklaşımlar, Yeni Yorumlar ve Yeni Kronoloji, Bilgin Kültür ve Sanat Yayınları (Ankara 2017).

Tümer 2017
H. Tümer, Van Hakkari Dağlık Bölgesi Kaya Resimleri (İstanbul Üniversitesi Sosyal Bilimler Enstitüsü, Tarih Anabilim Dalı, Eskiçağ Bilim Dalı, Yayınlanmamış Yüksek Lisans Tezi, İstanbul 2017).

Observations on the Urartian Economy in Light of the Excavations at Ayanis Castle

Mehmet Işikli – Oğuz Aras

Introduction

Before the Urartian Kingdom established a political unity in Eastern Anatolia, the tribes ruled in the region provided a strong basis for the economic structure of the kingdom. Unquestionably, the main subjects of this basis were agriculture and animal husbandry. Nomadism and semi-nomadism appears to be a form of livelihood that the East Anatolian region has forced on the settlers in this region since the Bronze Ages.[1] The Urartian Kingdom gathered all overlords (beys) in the 9th century and established the first political unity in Eastern Anatolia. The Kingdom protected the economic condition of these overlords and strengthened the system with new reforms. During the most powerful period of the kingdom, the borders of the lands reached to the Euphrates River in the west, Lake Urmiye in the southeast, Erzurum-Kars plateau in the north and Lake Sevan in the northeast.[2] The Urartian Kingdom built magnificent castles to provide central authority in this challenging geography and built external cities for the people who will serve these castles. According to Yakar, in the Urartian Kingdom, which had "a feudal monarchy", the ruling king was the one who directed the state policies.[3] Therefore the king himself was leading the economic policies. In general, giving a framework of the Urartian economy, we can say that under the king's hierarchy there were the members of the palace and the commanders who governed "Agriculture – Livestock, Reconstruction, Mining and Loot Taxes".[4]

Agriculture and Animal Husbandry

When the location of the fortresses built in the Urartian Kingdom were observed, the proximity to agricultural lands, water, natural resources and the control of the transportation roads were found out to be the main factors for selecting these locations.[5] The proximity to agricultural lands is one of the leading reasons.[6] The plain of Van, which includes the capital of Tushpa, is one of the most productive agricultural areas in the region. It is one of the largest lowlands on the shore of the lake in the region and Hoshap River flows through it.[7] Since the Gürpınar Plain, where the Castle of Çavuştepe is located, was a rich land in water resources for secondary agriculture, it attracted the attention of Sarduri II.[8] Furthermore, Aznavurtepe and Körzüt Castle, which are on the Patnos and the Muradiye Plains accordingly, are examples of fortresses that controls the agricultural areas.

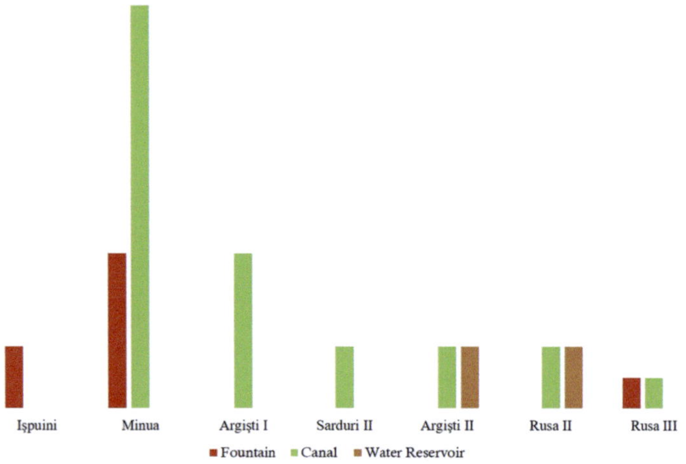

İşpuini	**Zivistan/Van** **Pirabat/Ağrı**
Minua	Van (4) Bekri / Muradiye Salmanağa / Erciş Adalar / Malazgirt Kotanlı / Malazgirt Karahan / Muradiye Yukarı Anzaf / Van Ain-e Rum / Ushnu Van Kalesi / Van
Argişti I	Surb Sahak / Van Van Kalesi (2) Karakala / Armavir Sardarabad / Armavir
Sarduru II	Ortadamla / Van Çavuştepe / Van
Argişti II	Çelevibağı / Erciş Hagi / Erciş
Rusa II	Gövelek Keşiş Gölü Savacık
Rusa III	Kaleköy / Mazgirt Zvartnos / Yerevan

Fig. 1: Water facilities of Urartian kings.

Despite these vast plains, dryland farming was not sufficient for a growing kingdom in this area. For this reason, from the emergence of the kingdom until its fall, every ruling king gave importance to the irrigation systems such as dams, canals and ponds (fig. 1). One of the largest and most famous of these water canals is Minua's canal. King Minua's canal had a length of about 55 km.[9] The only way to control the population, which was growing equally with the kingdom, was to give them the land they could cultivate.[10] Moreover, the way to use these fertile soils productively was irrigation systems. In Rusa's (son of Argishi) Keşiş Gölü inscription,[11] two important saying are noted: "Everyone was given bronze tools by Biani and foreign people". Considering the written sources, we concluded that apart from fields for planting, vineyards and the orchards had been highly important.[12] Unlike the plantations, the orchards and the vineyards had been pompous and more like gardening practices.[13] However, if we consider that most of the vineyards were used in wine production and that wine was an offering to the gods as libation, we can say that the vineyards are significant for the kingdom (fig. 2).

In the plateaus of Eastern Anatolia, the agriculture and the animal husbandry emerge as an inseparable economic model. The transhumance prevailing in the pre-kingdom region had not completely disappeared and survived with the kingdom.[14] The animals that spent the winter months in the barns or in the areas where the snow had fallen less were moved to the high plateaus/pastures in order to save crops in the summer.[15] If the written sources on Urartus are examined, we can see that animal husbandry holds an important place for the economy of the state. The Meher Kapı inscription, which was made in the period of Ishpuini and Minua and formed the basis of the Urartian

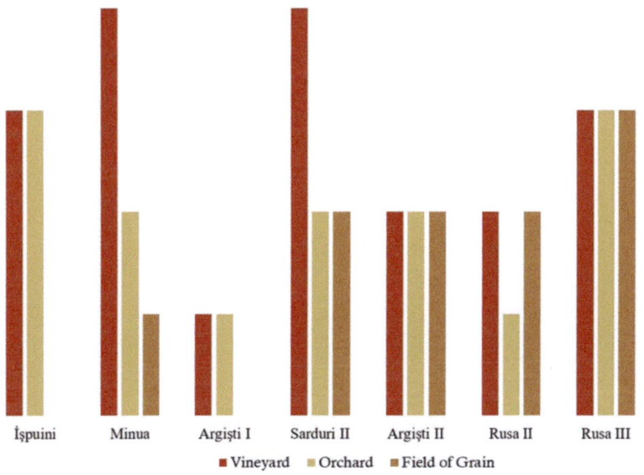

İşpuini	**Zivistan/Van Karahan/Muradiye Meher Kapı / Van**
Minua	Van Karahan / Muradiye Anzavurtepe /Patnos Güsak / Köşk
Argişti I	Sardarabad / Armavir
Sarduru II	Karataş / Erciş Armavir Armavir Çavuştepe
Argişti II	Çelevibağı / Erciş Hagi / Erciş
Rusa II	Gövelek Keşiş Gölü Savacık / Van Ayanis Kef Kalesi
Rusa III	Zvartnos / Yerevan

Fig. 2: Urartian kings and their agricultural projects.

religion, mentions the name of 79 god and goddess, and the number of sacrifices to be offered to these gods and goddesses in the religious ceremonies. The list begins with 17 bulls and 34 sheep in the name of Haldi, the chief god of the Urartian pantheon, and it decreases depending on the importance of gods and goddesses.[16] In the inscription of Keleshin belonging to the common kingdom, it is cited that 1.112 cattles and 21,600 sheep were sacrificed.[17] According to the archaeological data, approximately 500,000 animal bones and 1240 bulla have been found in a 15 ´ 4.5 metres room during Bastam Castle excavations. These bones are thought to belong to approximately 1500–2000 animals.[18] About 100,000 animal bones and 7 bulla were found under the ground. This data is very important in terms of giving us the number of animals consumed in the inner castle. Similar context, which include a lot of animal bones has been found during the recent works in Ayanis Citadel and it will be mentioned below.

Buildings in the Storage Area

In the region within the boundaries of Urartu, the geographical conditions limit the crops and the crop collection periods. Most of the products gathered from the agricultural activities could only be carried out in a single season and had to be stored. A part of the grain produced in a year was allocated to the feeding of animals, while the rest was kept in the storages for human consumption.[19]

We know that almost all of the cities built by royal command were constructed in a planned method considering the land structure. When we look into the distribution and the space of the storage areas within the citadels, we can argue that these areas are

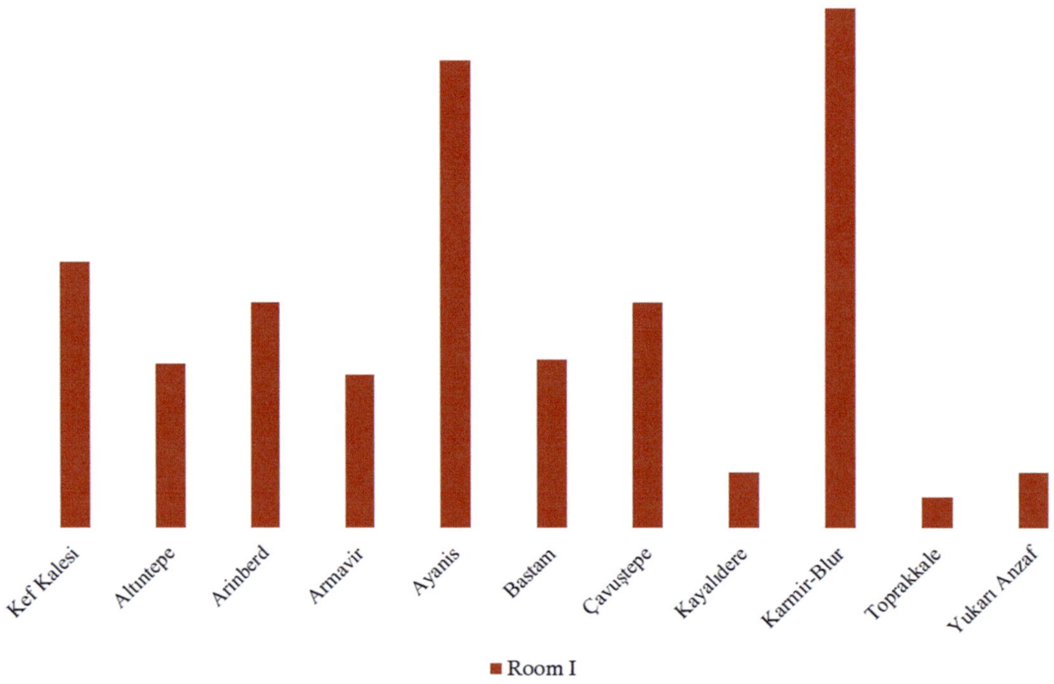

Fig. 3: Storage facilities with pithoi from Urartian sites.

clearly among the most important structures in city plans. From the gigantic dimensions of the pitos in the storage buildings, it is thought that firstly the pitos were placed in the area, and then the walls and gates of the storage structures were constructed.[20] (fig. 3).

Although the design of the storage rooms varies according to the structure of the land, they are basically long-narrow-planned structures built on the surface of the upper floors. By using the ground floors of the buildings, it was hoped that the crops would survive for a long time without being spoiled, and it would save space within the citadel. The pots and bowls that facilitate the transfer of goods to large pitos are among the other materials in the storage areas.[21] The volume of these pitoi and pottery in the storage rooms and the types of crop inside them are explained with cuneiform or hieroglyphs.[22] The only storage structure without pitoi has been found in Karmir Blur. On the floor of storage room 12, a heap of wheat in size of 25–45 cm has been found.[23] Driven by the Yoncatepe and Giriktepe storage structures, it is possible to say that large-sized storage structures are not only made by the king, but also by the overlords who were in charge of local governments.[24]

Booties and Taxes

The need for raw materials and manpower increased as a result of the expansionism since the early period of the kingdom. The only way to answer these needs was to

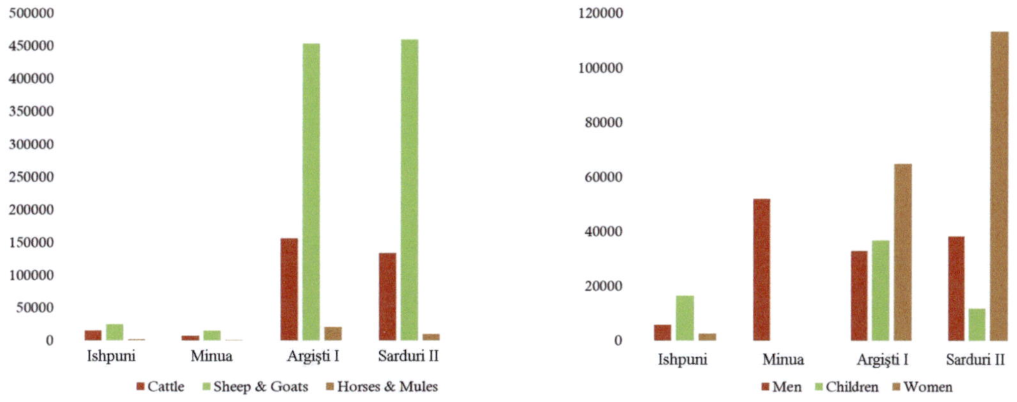

Fig. 4: The list of booty of humans and animals.

establish a colonial policy by using military force. According to the sources on Urartus, we notice that they took taxes from the local governments, which were under the control of Urartu kingdom, and campaigned against the rebellious states and held them for ransom.[25] Booties and the taxes were the most important source of income for the state (fig. 4). The countries such as Diauehi, Etuini and Mana, which did not hold any military threat, were always among the first countries on the list of campaigns. Although these campaigns are not very detailed in the inscriptions, the amount of booty, people, mines and animals are reported. Argişti, the son of Minua, speaks in the Horhor Inscription about the destruction of many countries / cities and how he took 52,675 people, including 19,255 young people, 10,141 alive warriors and 23,280 women as prisioners and killed some of them. Additionaly, 1,104 horses, 35,015 cattle and 100 thousands of livestock were seized.[26] If we propose that the numbers given in the inscription are the amount of the captives and the spoils in that year, we can reach the statistical data of the income gained from the campaigns. Considering that the amount of the spoils in this and similar inscriptions goes accordingly in an order of importance, "the man" has been the most valuable booty in human history.

The campaigns organized against the great powers such as Assyria were rare. Rusa the son of Sarduri mentions in his inscription of the campaign that he attacked Assyrian cities and defeated[27] them with the support of the king of the city of Ardini.[28] However, there is not any information about the booty and captives. We can claim that this campaign was organized in order to protect the city of Ardini, which was a border city between Assyria and Urartu, by interpreting the "After this, the peace is brought to the south " written on the northern surface of the inscription. This kind of inscriptions shows that the Urartian Kingdom did not attack more powerful kingdom/cities unless it was necessary. This wise policy helped them to survive approximately a quarter of a century in this harsh geography.

The campaigns carried out by the kingdom were not only important because of its booty but also for controlling the trading routes. Urartu, that aimed to control trade

Name of Items	Numbers of Artefacts
Copper [bronze]	3,600 talents (108 tons)
Helmets, Shields	25,212
Lances, Spearheads	1,514
Swords, Daggers, Bows, Arrows, Quivers	305,412
Cauldrons, Water Jugs, Pans	607
Other	12

Fig. 5: Bronze artefacts taken by the Assyrian king Sargon II from Muṣaṣir's Temple and Mineral Deposits In Eastern Anatolia.

routes in the middle of the 8th century BC, must have used natural passages and valleys in the mountainous East Anatolia. Along with this, it is known that a systematic road was built in Bingöl region, which had rich mining potential.[29] The northern Syrian ports 'Tell Açana' and 'Al Mina' were the easiest way for Urartu to maintain relations with the western world.[30] Therefore, they targeted to control these roads reaching the gateways to the Mediterranean and thereby the control of these roads could be gained. These political steps taken by the Urartian Kingdom during the development period greatly affected the interests of its most important rival, Assyria, and retrogressed its opponent in the region as the second great power.[31]

Besides, the inscriptions provide important information about the rich metal resources in its booty. Sarduri II mentions that he exacted 40 mina of solid (?) gold, 800 mina of silver, 2000 copper shield and 1535 of copper bowl as a tribute after the campaign against the country of Qumaha.[32] The Assyrian king Sargon II plundered the monuments offered to the Mushashir Temple during his campaign to the State of Urartu. The booty collected was 25312 bronze shields – helmets – guns, 1514 bronze spears – spearheads, 305412 bronze daggers – quiver – arrows and 607 bronze bowls – pots.[33] Assuming these inscriptions are exaggerated, and provided that we consider all the booty captured is from one temple, the importance of metal objects in the economic structure of the Urartian Kingdom (fig. 5) is revealed.

Ayanis Castle and its Economic System

The Ayanis Castle is one of the most important castles of the Urartu era. The castle is located on the eastern shore of Lake Van across the Süphan mountain and includes the citadel and the outer city. The noble people and the government officials lived in the citadel, while in the outer city, the people brought from campaigns were sheltered.

Fig. 6: The Western Storage rooms of Ayanis Castle.

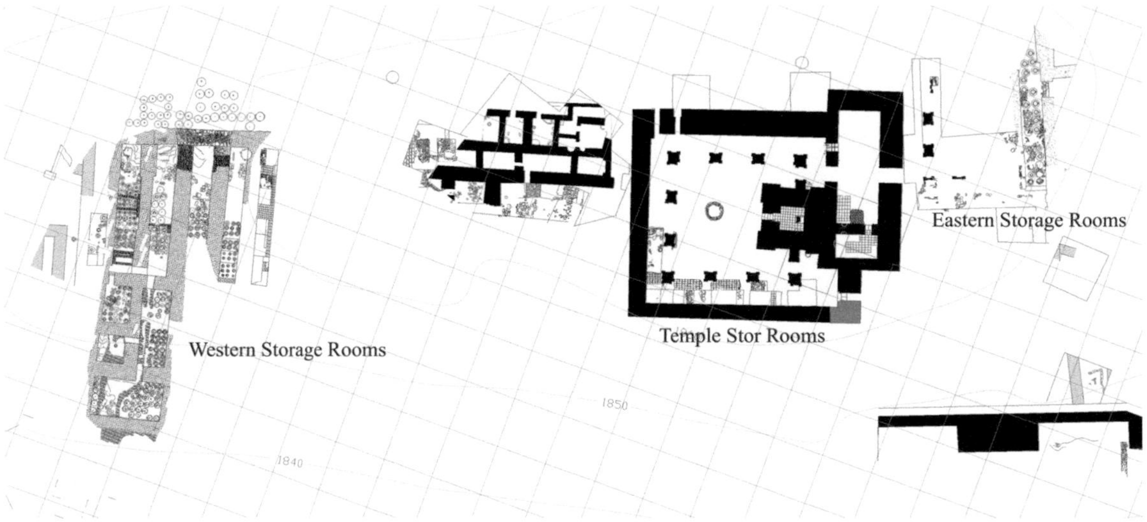

Fig. 7: Plan of Storage rooms in Ayanis Castle.

In the inscription of Ayanis Castle temple, Rusa, the son of Argishti, narrates that he used the people imprisoned from the enemy countries, among which were Assyria, for the construction of the castle.[34] The ethnic diversity of the population in the outer city that we know from the Ayanis Fortress and the agricultural equipment, which has been discovered during the excavations, are good examples that the written sources match with archaeological data.[35] This data clearly show the contribution of different ethnic groups to the state economy. Moreover, the tools distributed to the people are an indicator of an established economic policy.

The storage structures unearthed in the Ayanis fortress were spread over a large part of the castle. Basically, it is possible to mention 3 different storage structures. These are East Storage Rooms, West Storage Rooms and Temple Area Storages. The Western Storage Rooms cover an area of approximately 3,000 square meters. More than 200 large pitoi were recovered from these storage rooms (fig. 6). The size of these pithoi is 2.5 meters. In the Ayanis Castle room VI of the western storage, unlike other storage rooms, an earthenware pipe has been found. The transfer of goods to the outside might have been carried out more easily and faster through this pipe.[36] Many of these pithoi in the storages are covered with bullas. In these bullas information about where and how the goods are sent can be found. In addition, the signs on the pitoi indicate the capacity of the pitoi and what is inside. Based on this data, we can say that these storages are 'State Storages".

The storage rooms located on the eastern side of the castle and on the ground floor of the "Hall with Podium" vary in comparision to the Eastern Storage Rooms. No bulla has been recovered from the pithoi in this area. Furthermore, hundreds of pottery sherds have been collected on the lower floor of the same area. In addition to the 18 large pithoi, smaller vessels have been found. We can say that this smaller storage structure is different from the other state storages. Another storage area consists of storage rooms built beneath the temple area. In these storage rooms, bronze and iron artifacts were preserved (fig. 7).

The data on the animal husbandry of the Ayanis Castle was revealed in 2014 with the excavations. Thousands of animal bones and bullas were found under the soil just outside the north fortification walls. Very interesting and rich cultural contexts, which included animal bones, different finding, bullae and ash have been found on northern slopes of the citadel.[37] The animal bones from this context have been studied and results will be presented soon. Consequently, this context is very important in terms of showing the number of animals consumed in the given citadel.

Conclusion

As it is known the economic structure of Urartian Kingdom has been studied for some time. Avaliable data about this subject presented this picture; The use of animal husbandry, agricultural activities and raw material resources in the Urartian Kingdom is the core of the economy. Since the foundation years of the state, great fortresses have been built by giving importance to the constructions and the storages of these castles that have been filled for hard seasons. As we can see from the Urartian inscriptions, the kings, who ascended to the throne during the foundation years, frequently carried out campaigns on the chiefdoms. As a result of these campaigns, they played a major role in the growth of the state by capturing people and other spoils. Finally, also in some inscriptions, it is reported that a few chiefdoms were subjected to pay a tax to the state.

The excavations at Ayanis citadel, which have been countinuing for 30 years, have been enriching our knowledge about Urartu Kingdom and its economic structure. Monumental strorages with large capacities and many written documents, which have been found Ayanis citadel, are vital to understanding the economic system of this kingdom. Thanks to this data we are in a position to discuss this matter. Undoubtly, ongoing excavations at Ayanis citadel will be enlightening many unknown points related to this kingdom of the highland.

Notes

[1] Özfırat 2014, 26; Erdem 2018, 330.

[2] Çilingiroğlu 1997, 4–8; Salvini 2006, 24 f.; Köroğlu 2011, 12.

[3] Yakar 2011, 127.

[4] Sağlamtimur 2001, Lev. 42.

[5] For details see: Çevik 2009.

[6] Burney 2012, 55.

[7] Kalelioğlu 2018, 155 f.

[8] Çilingiroğlu 1997, 6.

[9] With the mighty power of God Haldi, Minua, the son of Ishuiu,has opened this channel. Its name is „Canal Minua". For details see: Payne 2006, 77.

[10] Sağlamtimur 2001, 39 f.

[11] UKN I, 268.

[12] UKN I, 268; Payne 2006, 286. I have set up fields, orchards and vineyards in my country.'

[13] Payne 2006, 81. 'This vineyard belongs to Minua's wife Tariria. His name is Tariria.'

[14] Çilingiroğlu 1997, 6.

[15] Sağlamtimur 2017, 4.

[16] Salvini 1994, 205–210; Çilingiroğlu 2011, 192–193.

[17] For details see: Salvini 2006, 55; Kuhrt 2013, 233 f.

[18] Kleiss 1980, 299–304; Kroll 2011, 163–167.

[19] Yakar 2011, 132.

[20] Çilingiroğlu 1997, 132.

[21] Çilingiroğlu 2001, 74. 82 fig. 11.

[22] For details see: Payne 2006, 331–338.

[23] Barnett – Watson 1952, 139.

[24] Çifçi 2017, 87 f.

[25] Payne 2006, 150–160. 208–240. 267–270.

[26] Payne 2006, 105.

[27] Payne 2006, 167 f.

[28] For details see: Işık 2015, 257 f.

[29] Belli 1977, 50. 102; Sevin 1989, 50 f.

[30] Çilingiroğlu 1984, 23.

[31] Piotrovskii 1969, 72.

[32] Çilingiroğlu 1997, 114; Payne 2006, 220; Salvini 2008, 426; Biber 2011, 234.

[33] Çilingiroğlu 1997, 114; Biber 2011, 234; Çifçi 2017,121.

[34] Payne 2006, 297.

[35] Stone – Zimansky 2004, 213–228; Stone 2005, 187–193; Piotrovskii 1966 205 fig. 8. 9.

[36] Çilingiroğlu 1996, 367; Çilingiroğlu 1997, 78; Çilingiroğlu 2001, 76 fig. 1.

[37] Işık – Işıklı 2015, 142–152.

Image Credits

Fig. 1–2. 4: Adapted by Çifçi 2017. – Fig. 3. 5. 7: Ayanis Castle Excavation Archive. – Fig. 6: Ayanis Archive.

References

Barnett – Watson 1952
R. D. Barnett – W. Watson, Russian Excavations in Armenia, IRAQ 14, 1952, 132–147.

Belli 1977
O. Belli, Urartular çağında Van Bölgesi Yol Şebekesi. İstanbul Üniversitesi Sosyal Bilimler Enstitüsü, Yayımlanmamış Doktora Tezi (İstanbul 1977).

Biber 2011
H. Biber, Urartu Silahları, Urartu: Doğuda Değişim, in: K. Köroğlu – E. Konyar (eds.), Yapı Kredi Yayınları (İstanbul 2011) 234–247.

Burney 2012
C. Burney, The Economy of Urartu: Probabilities and Problems, in: S. Kroll – C. Gruber – U. Hellwag – M. Roaf – P. E. Zimansky (eds.), Biainili-Urartu: the Proceedings of the Symposium Held in Munich, 12–14 October 2007, Acta Iranica 51 (Leuven 2012) 53–60.

Çevik 2009
Ö. Çevik, İskan Yeri Seçiminde Bilişsel Faktörlerin Olası Rolü: Rusa'nın Eiduru (Süphan) Dağı Önündeki Kent-Ayanis, in: H. Sağlamtimur et al. (eds.), Altan Çilingiroğlu'na Armağan. Yukarı Denizin Kıyısında Urartu Krallığı'na Adanmış Bir Hayat / Studies in Honour of Altan Çilingiroğlu. A Life Dedicated to Urartu on the Shores of the Upper Sea (İstanbul 2009) 195–202.

Çifçi 2017
A. Çifçi, The Socio-Economic Organisation of the Urartian Kingdom (Boston 2017).

Çilingiroğlu 1984
A. Çilingiroğlu, Urartu ve Kuzey Suriye, Siyasal ve Kültürel İlişkiler (İzmir 1984).

Çilingiroğlu 1996
A. Çilingiroğlu, Van Ayanis Kalesi Kazıları, 1993–1994 XVII. KST I. (Ankara 1996) 363–378.

Çilingiroğlu 1997
A. Çilingiroğlu, Urartu Krallığı Tarihi ve Sanatı (İzmir 1997).

Çilingiroğlu 2001
A. Çilingiroğlu, Storerooms. Ayanis I, Ten Years Excavations at Rusahinili Eiduru-kai 1989–1998, in: A. Çilingiroğlu – M. Salvini (eds.), Pubblicazioni dell'Istituto per gli Studi Micenei ed Egeo-Anatolici del Consiglio Nazionale delle Ricerche, Documenta Asiana 6 (Rome 2001) 67–84.

Çilingiroğlu 2011
A. Çilingiroğlu, Urartu Dini Yapısı, Urartu: Doğuda Değişim, in: K. Köroğlu – E. Konyar (eds.), Yapı Kredi Yayınları (İstanbul 2011) 188–205.

Işık 2015
K. Işık, Urartu Yazılı Kaynaklarında Geçen Yer Adları Ve Lokalizasyonları, Van Yüzüncü Yıl Üniversitesi Sosyal Bilimler Enstitüsü, Yayımlanmamış Doktora Tezi (Van 2015).

Işık – Işıklı 2015
K. Işık – M. Işıklı, Inscribed Bullae and Bone Layer Discovered at the Ayanis Fortress / Van in 2014, Altorientalische Forschungen 42, 2015, 142–152.

Kalelioğlu 2018
E. Kalelioğlu, Van Ovasının İklim Özellikleri, DTCF Dergisi, 2018, 155–166.
Kleiss 1980
W. Kleiss, Bastam, an Urartian Citadel Complex of the Seventh Century B.C., AJA 84, 1980, 299–304.
Köroğlu 2011
K. Köroğlu, Urartu Krallık ve Aşiretler, Urartu: Doğuda Değişim. in: K. Köroğlu – E. Konyar, Yapı Kredi Yayınları (İstanbul 2011) 12–54.
Kroll 2011
S. Kroll, İrandaki Urartu Şehirleri, Urartu: Doğuda Değişim, in: K. Köroğlu – E. Konyar, Yapı Kredi Yayınları (İstanbul 2011) 150–170.
Kuhrt 2013
A. Kuhrt, Eski Çağ'da Yakındoğu, C.2, Türkiye İş Bankası Kültür Yayınları (İstanbul 2013).
Payne 2006
M.R. Payne, Urartu Çivi Yazılı Belgeler Kataloğu, Arkeoloji ve Sanat Yayınları (İstanbul 2006).
Piotrovskii 1966
B.B. Piotrovskii, II Regno Di Van Urartu (Rome 1966).
Piotrovskii 1969
B.B. Piotrovskii, The Ancient Civilization of Urartu (Geneva 1969).
Sağlamtimur 2001
H. Sağlamtimur, Urartu Krallığının Ekonomik Yapısı Ege Üniversitesi Sosyal Bilimler Estitüsü Yayımlanmamış Doktora Tezi (İzmir 2001).
Sağlamtimur 2017
H. Sağlamtimur, Urartu Krallığı'nda Hayvancılığın Sosyo Ekonomik Açıdan Önemi, Anadolu Araştırmaları 20 (İstanbul 2017) 1–16.
Salvini 1994
M. Salvini, The Historical Background of the Urartian Monument of Meher Kapısı, Anatolian Iron Ages III. Anadolu Demir Çağları 3. The Proceedings of the Third Anatolian Iron Ages Colloquim Held at Van, 6-12 August 1990/ III. Anadolu Demir Çağları Sempozyumu Bildirileri Van, 6–12 Ağustos 1990, Ankara: The British Institute of Archaeology at Ankara (Ankara 1994) 205–210.
Salvini 2006
M. Salvini, Urartu Tarihi ve Kültürü, Arkeoloji ve Sanat Yayınları (İstanbul 2006).
Salvini 2008
M. Salvini, Corpus Dei Testi Urartei. Le Iscrizioni su Pietra e Roccia, Documenta Asiana 8 (Rome 2008).
Sevin 1989
V. Sevin, Urartular'a Ait Dünyanın En Eski Karayolu, Anadolu Araştırmaları 11, 1989, 47–56.
Stone – Zimansky 2004
E. C. Stone – P. Zimansky, The Urartian Transformation in the Outer Town of Ayanis, in: A.T. Smith – K. S. Rubinson (eds.), Archaeology in the Borderlands: Investigations in Caucasia and Beyond (Los Angeles 2004) 213 – 228.

Stone 2005

E.C. Stone, The Outer Town at Ayanis 1997–2001, in: A. Çilingiroğlu – G. Darbyshire (eds.), Anatolian Iron Ages 5, British İnstitute at Ankara (London 2005).

UKN I 1960

UKN I – G. A. Melikişvili, Urartsie Klinoobrazne Nadpisi 1 (Moscow 1960).

Yakar 2011

J. Yakar, Etno Arkeolojik Veriler Işığında Doğu Anadolu'nun Urartu Döneminde Sosyo-Ekonomik Yapısı, Urartu: Doğuda Değişim. in: K. Köroğlu – E. Konyar, Yapı Kredi Yayınları (İstanbul 2011) 126–148.

The Economic Conditions of the Eastern Anatolian Highland (Armenia Satrapy) during the Achaemenid Period

Leila Afshari – Soraya Afshari

A Glance on the Economic Structure in the Achaemenid Period

In the middle of sixth BC, the second Cyrus (the great) conquered a kingdom from Mede, Lydia, Babylonia, and the western Iranian plateau to the Mediterranean shore and also the eastern Iranian plateau in less than twenty years (550–530 BC). His successor, Cambyses, added Egypt to the kingdom in 525 BC. Later, in 518 BC, Darius conquered the India through the Indus riverbank and in 513 BC, paraded to the Scythia and subjugated the Aegean lands. Therefore, the development and expansion of the empire including the Oxus and Indus banks in the east to the Aegean and Mediterranean shore in the west, and from the Aral (Khwarazm) lake in the north to the Persian Gulf in the south was accomplished (fig. 1).[1] This extensive domain was consisted of the

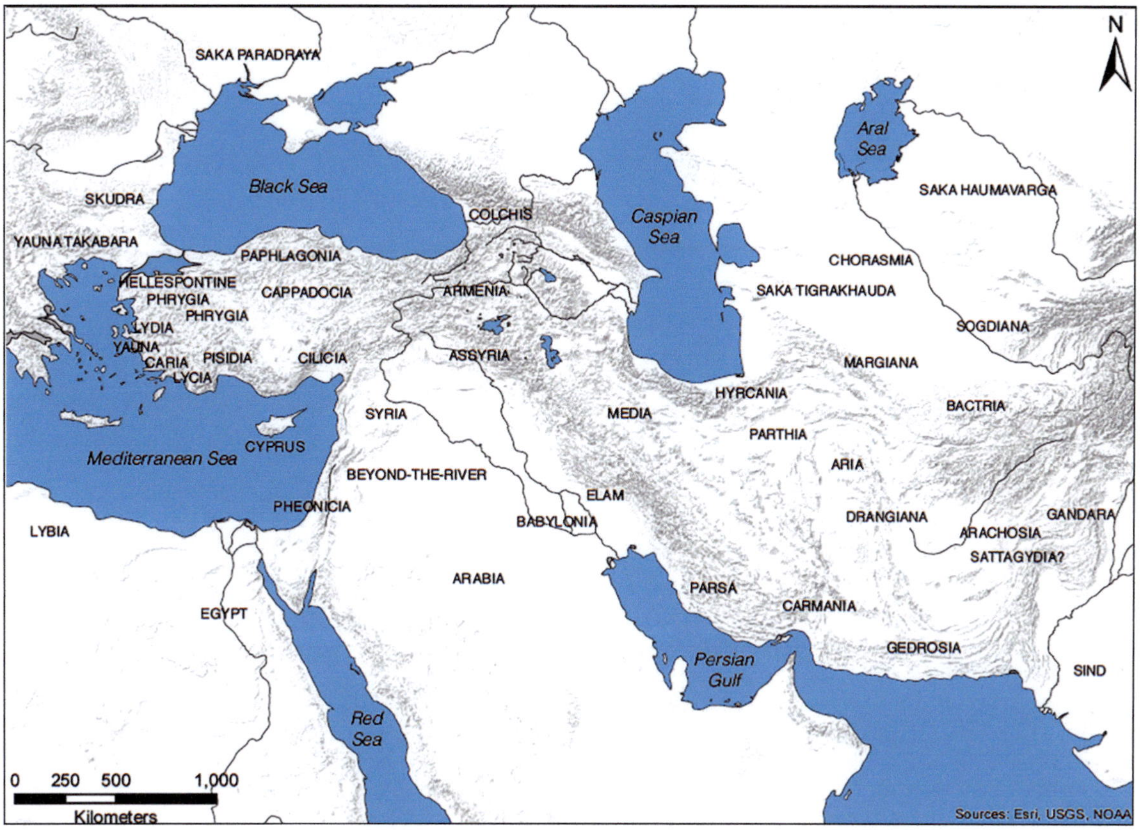

Fig. 1: The Achaemenid Empire.

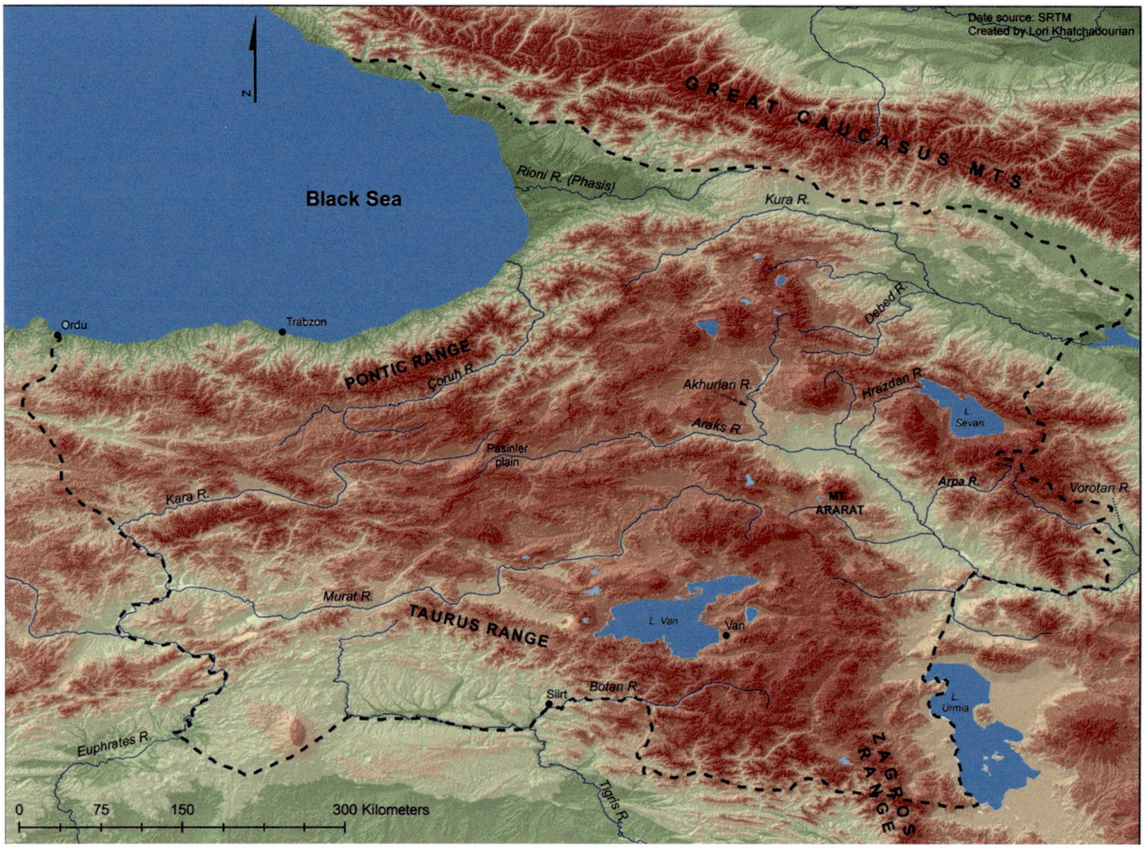

Fig. 2: Map of the highlands showing the borders of the "Main Satrapy Armenia".

different and various political-economical units. There are many Iranian names in the political-economical documents in other languages other than Old Persian to prove the point.[2] It can be said, about the economic structure of the Achaemenid Empire, as the political structure, it likely had some variety. Perhaps, it was a combination of different economies and, at the same time, an organized economic unit at the Achaemenid kings' disposal, who never forgot about the task of uniting this own political-economic unit. In the Achaemenid Empire there were various economic spheres combined. They rarely intervened in the economic and social life of their satraps. However, they provided the required military support and new opportunities for the development of economic relations and the exchange of their goods. The foundation of wealth in the Achaemenian Empire, and especially among the western satraps, were agriculture lands.[3] The Achaemenid Empire flourished due to the effective use of local elites and pre-existing institutions in each satrapy. Such was the case in Armenia, where the Achaemenid rulers used the former structures inherited from the kings of Urartu to serve Achaemenid imperial purpose.[4] Various sources suggest that the Achaemenid economic policy was based on encouraging more production, providing the necessary arrangements for the distribution and exchange of various goods and products among the satrapies and the economic freedom of these nations. The Achaemenid Empire did a lot of work within the satrapies to make them thrive in agriculture. Public works, especially the creation of irrigation canals, and so on, were used to flourish agriculture, and all this led to a rise in production in some countries and it brought about commercial prosperity in satrapies such as Armenia. During the Achaemenid rule, favorable and good conditions for the expansion of international trade were provided.[5]

Geographical Situation of the Satrapy of Armenia

The satrapy of Armenia is one of the more remote satrapies of the empire, stretching in the west from eastern Anatolia to the southern Caucasus Mountains and in the south to Lake Urmia. It is located quite a distance away from the center of the empire in Pars and creates the northernmost border of the empire in the southern Caucasus Mountains. Armenia has several natural borders such as the Black Sea to its northwest and the great Caucasus range to the north, the satrapy has a varied geography, containing mountains, plains, grasslands, semi-deserts, large lakes and several rivers and streams (fig. 2). The landscape is harsh and as a result the population was resilient. While the landscape was rough, it could also be plentiful: the numerous rivers and streams in the region left raw materials, especially metals such as copper, silver and iron.[6]

Role of the Satrapy of Armenia in the Economic System of the Achaemenid Empire

Land Transportation – Royal Road

The Persian Empire conquered lands that covered over 3.28 million square miles. So this Empire, as a superpower in the ancient world, needed a regular and efficient transportation system for the transmission of news, correspondence and messages, troops and relations with nations. Road construction in ancient times was based on military and governmental goals to facilitate the domination by the central government and the process of administrative affairs. In the aforementioned era, the cobblestone was developed as one of the road-building methods. The motifs carved on tablets and inscriptions confirm that vehicles, especially chariots and carts, were an integral part of people's lives.[7] In the Achaemenid period, trade, both within the empire and outside of it, developed on a scale previously unknown. It is evident that overland trade was being carried out using caravans. The Persians established an advanced road system. The Persians Royal Road, which was among the most important ones, perhaps the major one. It was probably established on a transportation network remaining from the Assyrian period. As the Persians expanded their area of domination towards the west, the part of the road network situated to the west of the Kızılırmak must have

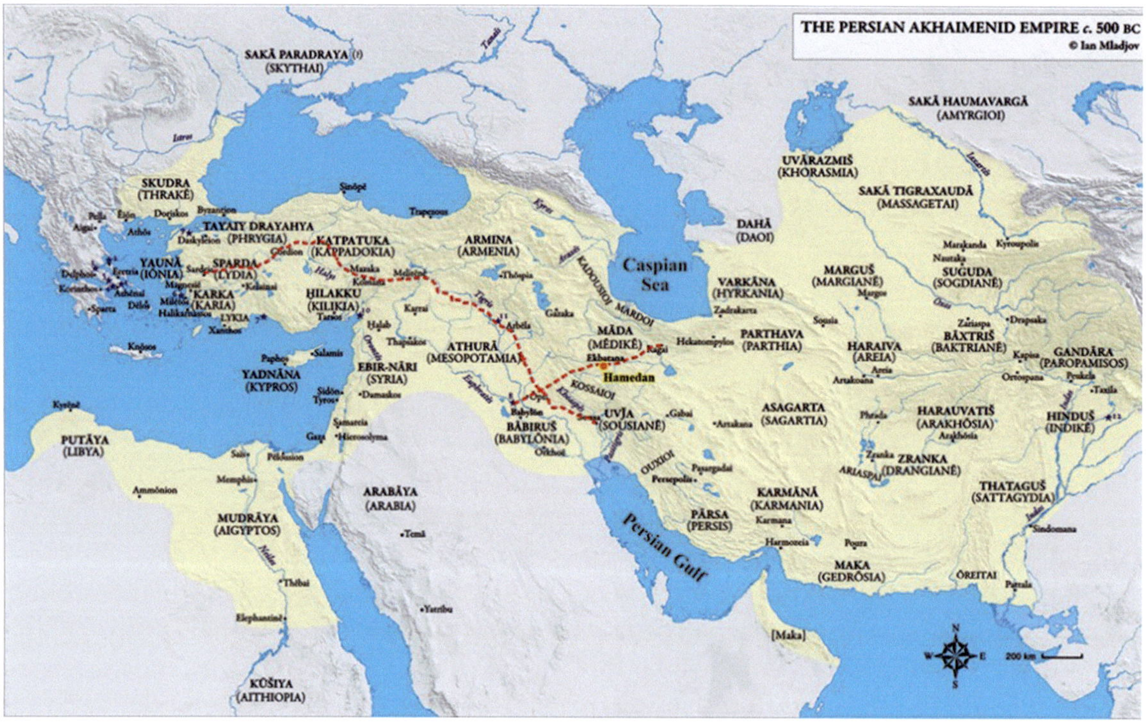

Fig. 3: The Persian Royal Road.

been restored. Although there is no precise evidence, the construction of the Royal Road, which connected the east to the west, by fixing the stopovers on the road, must have begun during the reign of the Persian king Cyrus. The construction must have been completeted during the period of Darius, when the satrapies were reorganized. Susa, which was the capital during the period of Darius, was thus connected to the old Lydian capital Sardis by a 2500 km long road. In addition to Susa, Persepolis was another city where western products would enter and where market traffic was heavy. There were stations every 25–30 km for the caravans to rest. The road, which was not only used for the transportation of people between east and west, but also for military and trade purposes, was referred to by Herodotus as the "Royal Road" (fig. 3).[8] According to Herodotus, part of the Royal Road passes through the Armenian Satrapy:

"In Armenia the resting places are 15 in number, and the distance is 56 1/2 parasangs. There is one place where a guard is posted. Four large streams intersect this district, all of which have to be crossed by means of boats. The first of these is the Tigris;....".[9]

Part of the Royal Road that crossed Armenia was probably in the plain of Xarberd and near the present day Melitene. In any case, the crossing of the Royal Road increased the value and strategic importance of Armenia and Cappadocia. In the Achaemenid period, the Royal Road had a very favorable and undeniable effect on the economic development of southwestern Armenia.[10]

Fig. 4: Armenian delegation on the eastern stairway of the Apadana at Persepolis.

The Role of the Armenian Satrapy in Tax Payment

In the satrap system of the Achaemenian Empire, the tax, which each satrap had to pay annually, was determined. During this period, the economic resources of people were taken into account, so that they could pay their annual tax and this was an important issue.[11] During the Achaemenian period, the most important part of these taxes included precious metals, agricultural products and livestock.[12]

There were two types of taxes taken from the satraps in the tax system of the Achaemenes. One was the tax calculated based on silver and was collected annually. The other was the tax collected based on agricultural and livestock products such as wheat, oats, horses and sheep. At the geographical kingdom of the Achaemenes, nearly all the satraps offered precious and different gifts to the king in addition to the annual tax in order to have good political relationship with the capital. Offering gifts was also done for another purpose. The satraps did it to have the support of the king. It also may mean that the Achaemenes kings always had dominance over their satraps.[13]

The Satrapy of Armenia was one of the main capital and financial sources of the Achaemenes Empire due to having natural resources such as mines, fertile soil and

Fig. 5: Erebuni Site.

permanent rivers.[14] Herodotus records Armenia's tribute obligation as 400 talents of silver,[15] while Xenophon[16] and Strabo[17] further attest payment in the form of horses. Xenophon states that the horse tax was differentially distributed according to a quota system across the villages of the *dahyu*. The village Xenophon visited had to supply 17 colts each year to local leaders, who transferred them to the satrap. The satrap would in turn pass them over to the court. Strabo notes that the *dahyu* supplied the king with 20,000 foals each year, which would be sacrificed in a festival to honor the god Mithra.[18] In addition to what was mentioned above, whenever the Achaemenes king passed Armenia, people offered him precious gifts.[19] The Apadana relief at Persepolis vividly represents this seemingly consensual inflow of silver vessels as no mere obligatory payment of debts but a spectacle glorifying sovereignty itself (fig. 4).[20] Furthermore, in 1968, in the course of construction activities at the foothill of Erebuni, located in the eastern highlands, about 450 km east of Altıntepe (fig. 5),[21] workers made on an astounding discovery: a hoard of five silver vessels, *deliberately flattened*, and inserted into a "big jug" (fig. 6).[22] They provide further evidence for the close association between Armenia and horses. Indeed, if the testimony of the Greek written sources is taken at face value, the horse rhtya from Erebuni would seem to symbolically unite into single objects, the *dahyu*'s twin tributary obligations of silver and horses.[23] Babken Arakelyan, the first to publish the Erebuni hoard, suggested that the vessels were flattened and stuffed into the ceramic jar in haste, in a moment of crisis—an impending raid, perhaps, in the heady closing years of

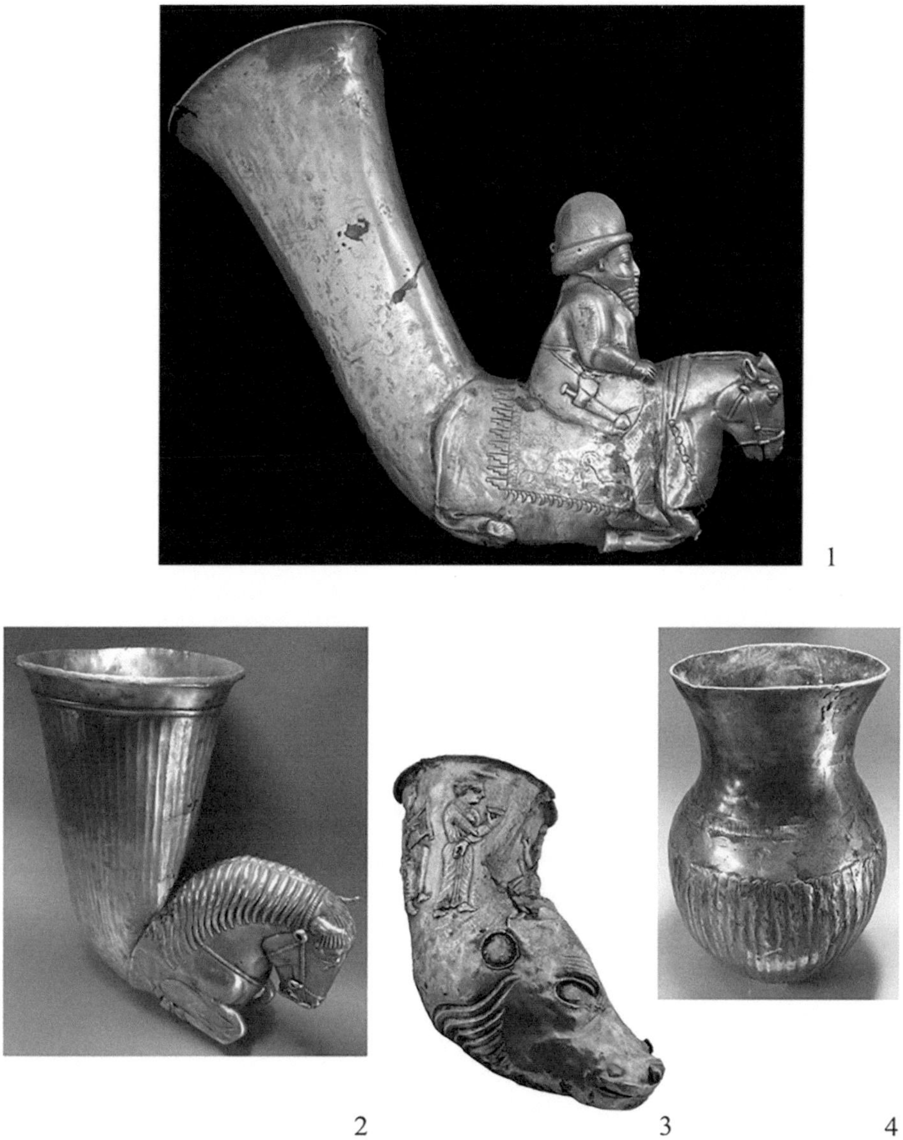

Fig. 6: Erebuni silver vessels , shown at comparable scale. 1. Horse-with-rider rhyton; 2. horse rhyton; 3. calf-head rhyton; 4. goblet rhyton.

the empire. Lori Khatchadourian also says, during one crisis, silver jewelry is likely to be placed inside this jug. It is also said that the flattened condition of the vessels (given what is known of hacksilver) suggests being less a scramble to sequester than the deliberate removal of silver from contexts of consumption and its forced entry into a new phase as monetary instruments. In any case, this much is clear: the vessels' silver properties thrust users at Erebuni into the same dependencies, material flows, and regulatory mechanisms that bound imperial agents elsewhere. The privileged actors of the Armenian highland who may have acquired and used these vessels, were ensnarled in regimes of value that shaped the Achaemenid economy and were based in large measure on the affordances of silver.[24] The vessels from the highland helped make the multidirectional silver flows that powered the material and symbolic economy of the empire possible. They imbricated their users in the cycles of tribute, gifting, royal redistribution, and imperial dependency on silver that materially reproduced the Achaemenid Empire. Many have argued for the abundance of argentiferous lead ores in Anatolia and in Armenia, suggesting that these regions may have been major sources for Achaemenid silver production. Most scholars conjecture that the Erebuni vessels were produced of these regions, usually offering more localized points of manufacture within that expanse, but strong evidence is in most cases not available.[25]

The Role of the Satrapy of Armenia in Agriculture and Animal Husbandry of Achaemenid Period

The Armenian Satrap also had a significant impact on the economy of the Achaemenid period, in terms of animal husbandry and agriculture. Herodotus believes that the presence of fertile pasture in Armenia has led to the cultivation of a number of livestock, among them breeding horses and camels had particular importance.[26] The signs of animal husbandry and agriculture in Armenia can be found in the findings from the excavation of Tsaghkahovit site.

The Tsaghkahovit Plain is a small, high-elevation plateau bounded on the south by Mount Aragats (4,090 masl), on the northeast by the slopes of the Pambak Range, and on the west by Mount Kolgat (fig. 7).[27] As a result of excavations, a lot of animal bones have been discovered, identified and analyzed in Tsaghkahovit. Sheep constitute the largest percentage of the number of identified specimens (NISP) identified to genus (48%), followed by cattle (39%). There are higher proportions of domesticated livestock in the Iron III sample than in samples from earlier periods on the Tsaghkahovit Plain. The third most represented taxon is *Equus*, of which the most common in the sample is the domesticated horse (*Equus caballus*) (1.53% of NISP identified to genus). It is worth noting that, according to Xenophon and Strabo, the Armenian satrapy paid its tribute to the Achaemenid court in the form of horses. The very limited evidence for burning (0.72%, a single astragalus) and butchery (0.72%, a single second phalanx) on the horses' bones suggests that perhaps most of these animals were not consumed but raised for use as transportation. By the mid-first millennium BC in southwest Asia, although horses were occasionally consumed, their primary purpose was probably for transportation.[28]

The importance of horses in the local economy at Tsaghkahovit was likely even greater than the faunal record suggests. It is certainly possible that the Tsaghkahovit economy was partially structured around the rearing of horses in order to pay taxes to satrapal authorities, who in turn fulfilled a tribute quota. Pigs and horses were

Fig. 7: Photograph of the Tsaghkahovit outcrop from the northwest.

also important elements of the Tsaghkahovit economy in the Iron 3 period. Horses, including domesticated taxa (*equus callabus*), comprise the fourth most common genus in the faunal sample and are more heavily represented than in any other period on the Tsaghkahovit plain. Sheep, goat, cattle, and pigs were major foci of the Tsaghkahovit productive economy in the Iron 3 period. It is likely that the small rooms in the heart of the settlement would not have accommodated the numbers of animals raised by the community. Sheep, goat, and cattle would also have supplied the community with other essential goods such as wool and dairy products. Tsaghkahovit's productive economy in the Iron 3 period appears to have been based on mixed agro-pastoralism. Tending to sheep, goat, and cattle was an essential part of daily life for part of the community.[29] Augmenting a diet of sheep, goat, cattle, and other animal products was a range of cultivated grains. Of the analysis of collected samples, 66 samples of the remains of the plants cultivated in this area have been identified. Wheat and barley are of the most cultivated species. As a result of the research, it is likely that millet, lentils and grapes were also cultivated in this area (fig. 8).[30] Discovering a great change among the clay findings of this site showed that agricultural commodities have been stocked in significant amounts in some parts of the region. It is possible

Fig. 8: Examples of archaeobotanical finds from Tsaghkahovit: 1. grain of cultivated hulled barley; 2. grain of tetra- or hexaploid wheat; 3. grain of emmer; 4. naked grain of broomcorn millet; 5. pip of cultivated grape; 6. nutlets of rose hip; 7. mericarp of *Galium* cf. *spurium*.

that these goods would be used for cold seasons, as well as for trading and selling to other parts of the Empire.[31]

Conclusion

Most of evidence indicates that the Achaemenid Empire took important steps to eliminate economic obstacles such as trade barriers within the kingdom. The result of this wise economic policy was the massive wealth flowing from satrapies like Babylonia and Armenia into the Achaemenid treasury. Persians, in addition to the vast commercial and economic support of the Armenian satrapy, also provided ground for facilitating other economic activities. In the meantime, major economic advances took place among the nations of the Achaemenid Empire, including Armenia. With the development of agriculture, Armenian exchange also increased with neighboring territories, which resulted in economic development. Growth in production has led to the promotion of general welfare in the Armenian Satrapy. The heavy tax, which Armenia was obliged to pay to the Achaemenid government, suggested that the land was economically in a special position and was one of the most important sources of supplying financial costs to the Achaemenid government. The Achaemenids needed experts and cheap human force, suitable raw and basic material for construction infrastructures to develop their Empire, the western satraps were rich of such. In order to meet this purpose, that is to reach the western satraps, the Achaemenid had to dominate the free seas and western business ways. The Achaemenid's dominance over these satraps developed the economic system of the Achaemenid to a new stage, which can be called the transnational economy. Finally, it must be said that,the ancient Armenian governments had political and economic ties with the Achaemenids. Therefore, achievements of the Achaemenid era were important for political, cultural and economic reasons.

Notes

[1] This subject has been discussed more comprehensively in Turkish in L.G. Gökçek – E. Yildirim – O. Pekşen, Economic and Agricultural Life in the Ancient Ages of the Anatolia (Istanbul 2018) 459–544. – Imanpour 2010, 87; Brosius 2006, 20.

[2] Dandamayev 1997, 101; Tavernier 2007, 2.

[3] Wiesehöfer 2009, 79.

[4] Soleymanzadeh 2018, 73.

[5] Diakonoff 1969, 297.

[6] Bocchieriyan 2016, 4.

[7] Soleymanzadeh 2018, 78.

[8] Tekin 2017, 130.

[9] Hdt.

[10] Soleymanzadeh 2018, 79f.

[11] Sarıkaya 2016, 76.

[12] Hallock 1969, 254–259.

[13] Duran 2015, 74 f.

[14] Ceylan 2015, 4.

[15] Hdt. 3.93; Briant 2002, 391.

[16] Xen. an. 4.5.3.34.

[17] Strab. 11.14.9.

[18] Khatchadourian 2016, 217.

[19] Durant 1964, 519.

[20] Khatchadourian 2016, 220.

[21] Khatchadourian 2008, 403.

[22] Arakelyan 1971, 143.

[23] Khatchadourian 2016, 129.

[24] Khatchadourian 2016, 134 f.
[25] Khatchadourian 2016, 135. 220.
[26] Parsamian 1963, 136–146.
[27] Khatchadourian 2014, 134. 139.
[28] Khatchadourian 2014, 163 f.
[29] Khatchadourian 2008, 285–287.
[30] Khatchadourian 2014, 163.
[31] Khatchadourian 2008, 288.

Image Credits

Fig. 1: Khatchadourian 2016, Map 1. – Fig. 2: Khatchadourian 2008, fig. 3.2. – Fig. 3: B. Balmaki, New evidence for the Achaemenid Royal Road in the Alvand Mountains (Hamedan, Iran), Antiquity. A Review of World Archaeology 90, 2016, fig. 1. – Fig. 4: Khatchadourian 2016, fig. 9. – Fig. 5: Google Maps. – Fig. 6: Khatchadourian 2016, fig. 29. – Fig. 7: Khatchadourian 2008, fig. 5.3. – Fig. 8: Khatchadourian 2014, fig. 20.

References

Arakelyan 1971
B. N. Arakelyan, Klad serebrianykh izdelii iz Erebuni. Sovetskaia arkheologiia 1, 1971, 1971, 143–158.

Bocchieriyan 2016
S. Bocchieriyan, The Achaemenid Satrapy of Armenia (Colorado 2016).

Brosius 2006
M. Brosius, The Persians (New York 2006).

Ceylan 2015
A. Ceylan, Ermenilerin Anadolu'daki Varlıkları ve Tarihi Gerçekler, in: Y. Topadoğlu (ed.), Trakya Üniversitesi Edebiyat Fakültesi Dergisi (Temmuz 2015) 1–30.

Dandamayev 1997
Encyclopedia Iranica 8 (1997) 101–104 s. v. Economy iii. in the Achaemenid Period (M.A. Dandamayev).

Diakonoff 1969
I. M. Diakonoff, Ancient Mesopotamia. Socio-Economic History (Moscow 1969).

Duran 2015
M. Duran, Satraplık Sisteminin Pers Yönetim Teşkilatındaki Yeri, SDÜ Fen Edebiyat Fakültesi Sosyal Bilimler Dergisi, Sayı 34, 2015, 61–86.

Durant 1964
W. Durant, Tarikh Tamadon, Tarjomeh Ahmad Aram, Entesharat Egbal, Jeld 1 (Tehran 1964).

Hallock 1969
R.T. Hallock, Persepolis Fortification Tablets (Chicago 1969).

Imanpour 2010
M.T. Imanpour, The Communication Roads in Parsa during the Achaemenid, in: M. Macuh – D. Weber – D. Durkin (eds.), Ancient and Middle Iranian Studies, Proceeding of the 6th European Conference of Iranian Studies, Held in Vienna 18–22 September 2007 (Wiesbaden 2010) 87–98.

Jamali et al. 2013
M. K. Jamali – N. Jadidi – A. A. Shahabadi, Nagsh va Jaygahe Satrapneshinhaye Garbi Iran dar Shahanshahi Hakhamaneshi (az 550–330 B.C), Daneshkade Adabiat va Olom Ensani Daneshgah Esfahan, Dore Jadid, Sale 5, Shomare peyapey 18, 2013, 89–110.

Khatchadourian 2008
L. Khatchadourian, Social Logics Under Empire: The Armenian ‚Highland Satrapy' and Achaemenid Rule, CA. 600–300 BC (PhD. diss. University of Michigan 2008).

Khatchadourian 2014
L. Khatchadourian, Empire in the Everyday: A Preliminary Report on the 2008–2011 Excavations at Tsaghkahovit, Armenia, AJA 118, 2014,137–169.

Khatchadourian 2016
L. Khatchadourian, Imperial Matter, Ancient Persia and the Archaeology of Empire (California 2016).

Parsamian 1963
E. S. Parsamian, Tarikh Mellete Armani, Entesharat Elmi Armanestan, Jeld 1 (Iravan 1963).

Sarıkaya 2016
S. Sarıkaya, Anadolu'da Pers Satraplık Sistemi, Akdeniz Uygarlıkları Araştırma Dergisi 4, 2016, 75–90.

Soleymanzadeh 2018
A. R. Soleymanzadeh, The Achaemenid Economic System and the Armenian-Georgian Situatio, ivane javaxiSvilis saxelobis Tbilisis saxelmwifo universitetis saqar Tvelos istoriis institutis Sromebi 13 (Tbilisi 2018) 70–87.

Tavernier 2007
J. Tavernier, Iranica in the Achaemenid Period (ca. 550–330 BC): Lexicon of Old Iranian Proper Names and Loanwords, Attested in non-Iranian Texts (Leuven 2007).

Tekin 2017
O. Tekin, Pers Döneminde Anadolu'da Para ve Ticaret, Persler Anadolu'da Kudret ve Görkem, Hazırlayanlar Kaan İren, Çiçek Karagöz, Özğün Kasar, Yapı Kredi Yayınları (İstanbul 2017) 102–135.

Wieshöfer 2009
J. Wieshöfer, The Achaemenid Empire, in: The Dynamics of Ancient Empires, State Power from Assyria to Byzantium (Oxford 2009) 66–98.

The Economic and Political Situation of Eastern Anatolia in the Classical Age

Nusret Burak Özsoy – Elif Yavuz

One of the names used often in history for the geography that is defined as the Eastern Anatolia Region today in Turkey, has been Armenia. The people of Armenia, taking a geography as a name for themselves, were among those who brought a gift to the king, which has been found in the famous Behistun inscription (520 BC) near Iran / Kirmanşah written during the reign of the Achaemenid ruler Darius (552–486 BC).[1] The first forms of the name Armenia are Arminiya, Arminiyaiy and Har-mi-nu-ya. The name "Arminiya" is considered the first record in this context. The identification is used for the 13th Persian satrapy, which was conquered later by Darius in the Achaemenid Empire.[2] Additionally, it is expressed that 400 talanton silver taxes were collected from the region in this period.[3]

Another source of information from ancient writers on the period of Persian domination in the region of Armenia belongs to Xenophon. In his work Anabasis, he gives information about the region's geography, the livelihoods of the ordinary people and their main occupations. Accordingly, the main livelihoods of the people living in Armenia are agriculture, livestock and horticulture. In the work, it is mentioned that Greek mercenaries under the command of Xenophon, who retreated Xenophon using the territory of the region, were able to supply agricultural and livestock products such as wheat, barley, dry beans, raisins, bacon, sesame, almonds, peanuts and peanut oil to almost every village. As well as beverages that were similar to beer and made from barley, high quality wines were also produced. Also, the Anabasis wrote down many pets such as goats, sheep, pigs, cows, chickens, horses. Strabo, on the other hand, mentioned that the Armenian lands, which were famous for their horses, had wide grasslands that were very suitable for horse breeding. He added that special war horses were raised for the Persian king in the region, the main horse supplier of the Persian army. In addition to these, the Armenian satrap sended 20,000 little horses to Persia every year for the Mithra festival.[4]

The first encounter between Alexander passing through Anatolia through Canakkale and the Persians was near Granikos.[5] Alexander defeated the Persians in the wars of Issos and Gaugamela[6], and conquered the whole region from Egypt to Kyrgyzstan. Alexander's conquest of Persia and his expeditions to the interior of India marked a new era in the economic life of Anatolia.[7] Conquests opened up new markets for Greek trade[8] and the balance of Greek and eastern trade radically changed with the provision of new raw material resources.[9] In the encounter of the Persians with the Greeks, the Armenians took part in the Persians' army and supported the Persians with horses and infantry.[10] However, our knowledge on the region of Armenia during Alexander and his Macedonian Kingdom is very limited. There is a bluff separation of ideas about how

Alexander pursued a policy in the region of Armenia. While some researchers stated that Armenia had no place in the conquest politics of Alexander,[11] on the other hand, other researchers agreed that Alexander had appointed Mithrines, the commander of Persians in Sardes,[12] as the satrap of Armenia.[13] However, there is no information about whether Mithrines controlled Armenia as a satrap. With the death of Alexander the Great in 323 BC, the military, political and economic constructions in the period before and after the Hellenistic period were divided into four parts: Mesopotamia and Syria were left to the rule of Seleukos. The dominance of Ptolemaios in Egypt, Libya and Levant regions; Lysimakhos in Thrace and Asia Minor, and Kassandros in Macedonia were seen.[14] Diodoros, who gave information about the state's share of the generals, did not mention Armenia.[15] However, Cappadocia, Armenia and Atropatenan are known to maintain their legal status within the Seleucids.[16]

Appianos declared that Armenia was attached to the Seleucid Kingdom during the reign of Seleucid I (305–281 BC).[17] However, as in the Persian period, the region never entered the Seleucids' direct dominance area during the Seleucids period.[18] The colonization activities of the Seleucids were different from the other kingdoms. For the Seleucids, the heart of the kingdom was Syria thus, they carried out their colonization activities in this region.[19] During the Seleucid period, the region was divided into three separate administrative regions: Greater Armenia, Sophene and Lesser Armenia. This distinction continued until the Byzantine period with some changes.[20] In Armenia, Sophene was the closest to the Hellenistic world, immediately bordered on the borders of Mesopotamia in the south and close to the main trade routes of northern Mesopotamia.[21] There was a trade route to Babylon through the Euphrates River coming from the western border,[22] and as previously mentioned, through the special rafts that Herodotus also described.[23] The region of Armenia never came into the intensive colonization area of the Seleucids. The rugged structure of the region and the unfavorable climatic conditions were perhaps the most important reason for this.

The internal turmoil that the Seleucid Empire, which was one of the successors of Alexander and a Hellenistic kingdom based in Antiocheia, experienced in the early 1st century BC led to the emergence of different powers in the dominance of this empire. Parths, Romans and Armenians were the main forces that emerged in the Seleucid Empire's sovereignty. While the change of political balances led to the emergence of new powers and new controversies, the economic problems were another reason for Rome to deal with the region. The dominant political power of Rome has felt the need for further attention with the political developments in the Roman region due to the increasing interest of patricians in the eastern world for various luxury consumer goods and exotic products.[24]

The transit trade road, known as "the Silk Road" (Seidenstraßen) between the east and the west, had two important centers.[25] One of them were the ports of the eastern Mediterranean and the other the ports in the Black Sea. An example of these ports in the Black Sea is the port of Tana at the mouth of the Don River, which is located on the coast of the Sea of Azov. Roads followed during the commercial activities were carried out in east-west direction. They ended in these ports.[26] The main commercial product carried by this road network, with different alternatives from land and sea, was silk. However, a wide range of products, such as lapis lazuli, jade stones, various spices, fabrics, ivory, exotic fruits and animals, were transported. These products from China and India appealed to the emperors, kings, nobles and people of the upper class in western markets. Especially silk was very valuable. It was seen that the Romans and the Parths engaged in an intense struggle in order to obtain the silk and other valuable goods coined with gold and to get more shares of the east-west trade.[27]

With the peace of Apameia, which was signed in 188 BC, Roman domination started in Asia Minor. The period between 189–10 BC are the years when the Artaksias dynasty was in power.[28] In 190 BC, with the emergence of Rome as the dominant power of the Mediterranean world, there was another force in the east, Parth.[29]

Along with these revolutionary changes in the geopolitics of the dominance zone of the Artaxias, Artaksias was recognized as an independent king in Armenia as a result of his alliance with the Romans. In addition to Rome, it was another force that recognized the dominance of Artakssi in Parth. Thus, some new administrative changes occurred in this new dynasty in the region of Armenia. A new administrative system and tax system was established with the new capital established on the Araxes River.[30]

It is known that at least ten new cities were built during the Artaksias dynasty. The most famous of these is Artashat (Artaxata or Artaxhsata), which is also the first independent capital of the Kingdom of Armenia. This city is located 24 km south of modern-day Erivan.[31] Cities, which were centers of foreign traders, mediated the spread of Greek cultural values. The 2nd and 1st century BC to the 3rd century BC is the period, in which the Hellenistic influences were strong. Together with the Hellenistic period, the growth of the money economy started a vibrant period of commercial life and industrial activity with the establishment of a number of Greek colonies and cities that had a strong influence on the cultural development of Asia Minor. Artashat, one of the most important cities built by Artaksias and the capital of the new dynasty, was the main political, administrative, economic and cultural center. The city, whose geographical location and the regional economy were important elements, and which dominated the trade routes, was easily accessible for international trade.[32]

Another important factor for the economy in this period was the temple economy. The cult of the temple, which is a common trend among kings and elites is that the temples dedicated to ancestors or gods have great properties and riches become a dominant element in the economy. Temple complexes were like a city center.[33]

The peasants in the lower classes had certain rights in the land where they work, but they cannot be said to receive the full value of their labor. As status, the peasants were free. However, they had to pay heavy taxes. The lowest part of society were slaves. Dynasty members, nobles and temples had many slaves. Thousands of people who were brought and enslaved from the occupied places by military service were an important labor force and economic value for the economy of the period. Slaves were used in the construction or maintenance of large public projects such as roads, canals, irrigation systems and cities by state. Slavery was, therefore, an important component of the economy.[34]

After the first king of Artaksias dynasty Artachsias I, Artavasdes I (160–115 BC) and Tigranes I (115–95 BC) dominated the sovereignty. In this period, however, the Parthans filled the authority gap which was experienced due to Rome's struggle with Carthage. The two kings who came after Artaksias I could not escape the influence of Parth.[35] When Artavasdes I was defeated by the Parth, his nephew was sent to Ctesiphon, the capital of Parth, as a hostage. It is understood that the Parths realized the importance of Armenia as a big trade center in this period. Especially the newly established capital of Armenia, Artashata, was an important stopping point in east-west trade. In this period, Artaxias founded a mint to further facilitate trade in Armenia.[36]

After the death of Tigran I, the king of Armenia, Tigranes II who washeld in Ctesiphon, was released, reciprocating this with a series of valleys in the Greater Armenia region to the Parths for his freedom,[37] then he became the new king of Armenia. Tigranes who remained in power between 97–54 BC, continued the expansion policy, which started in the period of Artaksias I.[38]

During the period of economic prosperity under Tigranes II, during which the kingdom of Armenia lived its most brilliant period, significant zoning-settlement activities were observed in the region. In the early 70s BC, II. A new capital was built in honor of the name of Tigranes further south because the old capital Artashata on the river Araxes stayed too far away in the north for governing the kingdom due to the expansion of Armenia's borders. We learn the most important information about this new capital city from Appianos. It also had a theater that resembled the Greek capital of the new capital, with large parks, hunting grounds and lakes.[39]

To populate the new city, half a million people, according to an estimation, from neighboring countries such as Adiabene, Assyria, Gordiene, Arabian Mesopotamia, from different ethnic backgrounds and Greek origin from small Asia were displaced and thus, a cosmopolitan structure was formed. These displaced people guided the commercial and industrial developments within the empire.[40]

The welfare and peace environment provided by Tigranes II in the region of Armenia was not prolonged. The imperialist side in the Roman senate moved in order to get rid of the king of Pontos VI., one of the greatest enemies of Rome, and impose its solution to the east.[41] Lucullus who defeated the king of Pontos, Mithridates, then marched on Armenia and King of Armenia also defeated Tigranes II in the Tigranocerta War.[42]

The Tigranocerta War can be described as a disappointment for the Kingdom of Armenia, which lived its most powerful and fully independent period in the 1st century BC. After this war, the imperial dreams of the Kingdom of Armenia ended.[43] By 68 BC, after capturing Tigranocerta, Lucullus made a number of unsuccessful attempts to seize Tigranes II and Mithridates VI to root out the matter.[44] After Lucullus failed, the Roman senate dismissed him and appointed Pompeius.[45] In 66 BC, Pompeius, who took over, quickly moved to protect the Roman sovereignty and economic interests in the east.[46] After the death of Tigranes II, Artavasdes II (55–34 BC) has passed. Artavasdes II tried to maintain the buffer state and balance policy between Rome and Parth.[47]

In this period, the crazier attempt of Marcus Licinius Crassus[48] against the Parths to gain more recognition decayed an about ten year peace signed by Pompeius and Phrates III between the Romans and the Parthian.[49] After Crassus' death in the Battle of Karrhai, the years 49–48 BC there was the scene of civil war between Caesar and Pompeius. Caesar who won this struggle in 47 BC was assassinated on March 15th in 44 BC without applying the unrealistic plan of invading Persia from Armenia in 45 BC, passing from the Caspian Sea to southern Russia and from there, via Germany, Gaul and returning to Rome.[50]

After the destruction of Caesar, the second Triumvirate (43 BC–38 BC) was founded in Rome, consisting of Marcus Antonius, Octavian (Augustus) and Lepidus.[51] Following the new Triumvirate, the Romans took action under the leadership of Marcus Antonius to avenge the defeat in Karrhai and restore the lost Roman reputation.[52] The army of Antonius moved in 36 BC. While the process before expedition for Antonius and the Roman army advancing under the supervision of Arvastes II went on succesfully, they failed due to Antony's tactical errors and the Roman army, despite its tremendous magnitude, suffered significant losses from its present with the withdrawal of Artavasdes II's support and took back by taking a heavy defeat.[53] In 34 BC, Antonius invaded Armenia and captured the king to take revenge on Artavasdes II, who let him down, and on his defeat.[54] On the other hand, the people of Armenia declared Artaksias II, the eldest son of Artavasdes II, as the new Armenian king.[55]

The region of Armenia became an obstacle for effective military actions between Rome and Parth sometimes with its own power, sometimes with its rugged topography and geographical features, sometimes together with both elements, the role of a buffer state, in this context, became an identity for the region. Therefore, both powers adopted a policy of keeping Armenia in the periphery of their territory. As a matter of fact, by abolishing the threat of Antony and Cleopatra, *Principatus*[56] in Rome and Augustus, who started the imperial period, tried to control Armenia region.[57]

Augustus was not pleased with the *status quo* of the East in 20 BC. He also wanted to recapture the Roman banners that had been captured by the Parths in the battle of Karrhai. Because this meant a great loss of prestige for Rome. In this direction, Augustus took the initiative to solve these problems to the East in 20 BC and the Roman banners that were captured after the defeat of Crassus took back by the agreement with the Parthians.[58]

After the agreement of the Romans with the Parthians during the period of Augustus, it was once emphasized that the Euphrates had been a border between the two powers. As a matter of fact, the state of the Euphrates being a natural border was also emphasized in the testament of Augustus that he left to his successors after his death. Because, in order to continue the existence of Rome in Anatolia, the Euphrates River had to be held and the Parths had to stay on the east side of this river.[59]

After Artaksias II, the reign of the Armenian King Tigran III (20 BC–10 BC) did not last long with Roman intervention. On the suspicion of betrayal of Tigran IV, the son of Tigran III, Augustus interfered in his power and Tiberius came to Armenia with Artavasdes III, a cousin of Tigran. This arbitrary movement of the Romans provoked a rebellion in Armenia with the incitement of the Parthians.[60] The power of Tigranes was recognised in consequence of the rebellion that was squashed by Romans and his reconciliation with Rome.[61]

After the death of Augustus in his 16 years, the Parth / Artaksias dynasty tried to break the dominance of Rome in Armenia and Mesopotamia. In this period, the new king of Armenia was Tridates who was the brother of Vologases I, the king of Parth. Tiridates I, who ruled intermittently on the throne of Armenia since 53 AD, ruled Armenia between the years of 62–75.[62] As a result of Parth attacks during the Roman-Parth period between the years 55–63 AD and Rome's loss of Armenia Roman authority was shaken in the region.[63]

In 58 and 63 AD an army was sent under the command of Cn. Domitius Corbulo to intervene in events in the region by the Roman emperor, Nero.[64] They devastated Tigranocerta and Artashat. Tiridates I took refuge in the Parths.[65] And Tigranes I was appointed to the throne of Armenia by Corbulo. But when Corbulo invaded Armenia for the second time in MS 63, Parthlar called for a ground of agreement. In 63 AD, the Rhandeia (modern Kharpert) Peace[66] was signed between Rome and Parth. According to this, the brother of Parthian king Vologases, Tiridates, would remain under the throne of Armenia, but would take the crown from Rome.[67] Thus, the Arsakes / Arshakid / Arsakuni dynasty, which was going to continue until 298 AD, started in Armenia[68] This period was perhaps the most important period of prosperity and superiority that the region had experienced since the Urartu Kingdom. The region, taking advantage of the limited commercial concessions, which were made with Rome increased importance in the second half of the 1st century AD when the Roman Empire was strengthened in Anatolia.[69]

The major Parthian expedition of Traian led to the conquests from Petra, the major commercial center in the west to Ktesiphon, the capital of the Parthian in the east and to Susa, the historic commercial center and the beginning of the king's road. After this expedition, Armenia became a Roman province and the Romans' historic rival in the east, Parth, was reduced to vassal kingdom status.[70] It is seen that the successes of Traianus were compromised during the reign of Hadrianus, the successor of Traianus. In 120 AD, the Roman armies in the region withdrew and the border was again designated as Euphrates.[71]

The struggles of the Empire of Rome with the Parthians continued until the establishment of the Sassanid State by eliminating the Parths under the leadership of Ardaşir / Artaxerses in the period of Septimius Severus Alexander, the Roman Emperor, (222–235 AD).

As a result, while the Eastern Anatolia Region, an important place in the strategic, commercial and political sense since the oldest periods of history, has provided the connection between Caucasus and Mesopotamia in north-south direction, it has also provided the connection of the roads to the inner parts of Anatolia and Asia in the east-west direction. As well as rich underground and ground resources, the Eastern Anatolia Region with its dominant position in Anatolia, has been the scene of fierce struggles between the Romans and Parthians who wanted to take control of the position of dominating the international trade routes, which have an important place in both the global and local economic system. Nevertheless, its rugged topography and harsh climate has not created attractive conditions for those who want to settle in this land; it has usually been in their periphery although it has been next to large cultural areas. In comparison to the west of Anatolia, the region lacks the traces of the architectural remains that ancient cultures have left behind. As a feature of its physical geography, it often has a fragmented political outlook, and since the Urartian Kingdom, there has not been a centralized power in the region, and its political control has been difficult. Within the scope of Roman-Parthian struggles, it was mostly in the buffer / vassal kingdom position an both powers were not included in the areas of strict control except for short periods. Therefore, the dominant power in the region has often changed. The Romans adopted the Euphrates River as a natural border and they were not willing to move to the east of the Euphrates except for short periods of rule. However, they did not neglect to keep these military forces alert through the north-south legions along the Euphrates River where they recruited their military forces against the danger of Parth in the east. The fierce struggle by the forces that dominated the region has brought profitable commercial activities as well as the destruction during the periods of peace. As a result, the struggle for welfare and prosperity flowing through the international transit trade route, which has passed to modern literature as the Silk Road has determined the economic and political fate of the Armenia region.

Notes

[1] This subject has been discussed more comprehensively in Turkish in a book titled "Economic and Agricultural Life in the Ancient Ages of the Anatolia" (Eds. L. Gürkan GÖKÇEK, Ercüment YILDIRIM, and Okay PEKŞEN), 2018, 459–544. – Frye 1984, 363.

[2] Schmitt 1987, 417.

[3] Tekin 2007, 47.

[4] Xen. an. 4.4.7.; 4.4.9.; 4.4.13.; 4.5.25.

[5] Martin 2013, 245.

[6] Redgate 1998, 62.

[7] Frank 2004, 62.

[8] Rostovtzeff 1936, 233; Manning 2014, 8.

[9] Before Alexander, in the 4th century, the Greek trade area was almost entirely limited to the Mediterranean or Black Sea coasts. Trade with Asia's interior regions was clearly only of secondary importance. However, after the conquest of Alexander by Persia, they were all radically changed. Trade has gained a worldwide character by attracting not only Asian Minors, Mesopotamia and Egypt, but also into the circle of live and direct commercial relations in the remote areas of Central Asia and India.

[10] Burney – Lang 1971, 187.

[11] Cook 1962, 162.

[12] Chahin 1987, 187.

[13] For details, see Hammond 1996, 130–137.

[14] Mamandian 1965, 204; Cook 1962, 161; Martin 2013, 255; Rolf 2011, 223–287.

[15] Diodoros Siculus,18.3.

[16] Mamandian 1965, 204; Mommsen 2005, 95; Rostovtzeff 1936, 237.

[17] Appianos 314, 55.

[18] Burney – Lang 1971, 187–191.

[19] Jones 1971, 242.

[20] Burney – Lang 1971, 191.

[21] Mamandian 1965, 205

[22] Casson 2002.

[23] Hdt. 1991, I.194.

[24] Keaveney 1992, 101; Demir 2014, 55.

[25] (Seidenstraßen); Richthofen 1877, 96–122; Litvinsky 1996; Warmington 1974; Liu 2010; Frankopan 2015.

[26] Hermann 1935, 26 f.; Warmington 1974, 18–34; Litvinsky – Guangda et al. 1996, 35.

[27] Warmington 1974, 105; Tezcan 2005, 3 f.

[28] Kurkjian 1964, 69; Garsonian 1997, 44; Strab. 11.14.5.

[29] Tezcan 2014, 156.

[30] Panossian 2006, 37.

[31] Kurkjian 1964, 70

[32] Payaslian 2007, 15; Lang 1983, 509; Manandyan 1965, 46–49.

[33] Payaslian 2007, 16.

[34] Payaslian 2007, 16.

[35] Diod. 31.17.; App. Syr. 45, 66.; Bournoutian 2006, 29 f.

[36] Bournoutian 2006, 29 f.

[37] Strab. 11.14.15; Justinus Epitome 1853, 38.3.; Debevoise 1968, 45

[38] Bournoutian 2006, 30; Kurkjian 1964, 74; Strab. 11.14.15; Plut. Lucullus 21–26.

[39] Garsonian 1997, 56; Kurkjian 1964, 76; Panossian 2006, 37; Jones 1998, 201; Çiğdem 2011, 97–118; Yavuz 2014, 2–4.

[40] Payaslian 2007, 20; Garsonian 1997, 56; Kurkjian 1964, 76; Panossian 2006, 37; Bournoutian 2006, 32; Payaslian 2007, 20.

[41] Garsonian 1997, 56; Plut. Lucullus 21.534/5. 538/9; Keaveney 1992, 102 f.

[42] Plut. Lucullus 23.7; Memnon 2007, 38.1; Cic. Manil. 23; Keaveney 1992, 103.

[43] Strab. 12. 3. 28, 30, 13. 1. 55; Plut. Lucullus 1914, 14,6–8. 21,2. 23,7. 27,7. 29,7. 30,1. 78. 43,2; Sherwin - White 1983, 174–176; Sullivan 1990, 97–99; Jones 1998, 224; Kaya 2004, 73–86; Tekin 2007, 141; Palaz Erdemir 2014, 3–6; Yıldırım 2016, 51–73.

[44] Plut. Lucullus 31; App. Mithr. 1912, 13.87.

[45] Eutr. 6.12; Cass. Dio 36.20; Cic. Manil. 27.

[46] Chahin 2001, 204.

[47] Chahin 2001, 204; Garsonian 1997, 60.

[48] Boak 1921, 184.

[49] Keaveney 1991, 66 f.; Redgate 1998, 76; Benjamin 1891, 163.

[50] Ball 2002, 14; Payaslian 2007, 24.

[51] Plut. Antonius 30; Bournoutian 2002, 34.

[52] Plut. Antonius 37.3; Colledge 1967, 43 f.; Huzar 1978, 173.

[53] Plut. Antonius 38; Strab. 11.13.4.; Cass. Dio 49,25–26; Vell. 2.82.3; Ball 2002, 107; Redgate 1998, 78.

[54] Cass. Dio 49.39.2.

[55] Cass. Dio 49.39.5.

[56] Momsen 2005, 73; Tekin 2007, 222.

[57] Sherwin-White 1977, 65.

[58] Cass. Dio 54.8.1–2; Suet. Aug. 21.3; Eutr. 7.9; Taylor 1936, 163; Gruen 1996, 159 f.

[59] Gibbon 1987, 23; Kaya 1998, 163; Momsen 1996, 95.

[60] Kurkjian 1964, 88.

[61] Cass. Dio 55.9.4–5; Cass. Dio 55.10.18; Tac. ann. 11.4; Vell. 2.101.1; Momsen 1996, 95; Swan 2004, 112. 125; Anderson 1934, 273–277; Campbell 1993, 222.

[62] Bournoutian 2002, 40.

[63] Wheeler 2011, 243.

[64] Shotter 2005, 38; Champlin 2003, 39.

[65] Benjamin 1891, 168; Shotter 2005, 38; Champlin 2003, 39.

[66] Garsonian 1997, 67.

[67] Champlin 2003, 221; Shotter 2005, 39.

[68] Tac. ann. 13,6. 13,34. 14,23.26. 15,1.17 15,24.31. 16,23.3; Cass. Dio 62,19.23; 63,1–6; Bournoutian 2002, 41; Garsonian 1997, 67.

[69] Tezcan 2014, 155 f.

[70] Akşit 1970, 186 f.; Gibbon 1987, 27; Frye 1984, 242.

[71] Campbell 1993, 215; SHA Hadr. 2.21.11; Gibbon 1987, 27.

References

Adontz 1946
N. Adontz, Historie d'Armenie Les Origines (Paris 1946).

Akşit 1970
O. Akşit, Roma İmparatorluk Tarihi (M.S. 193–395) (İstanbul 1970).

Anderson 1934
J. G. C. Anderson, The Revolt of Armenia and the Mission of Gaius Caesar, CAH 10 1934, 273–279.

Ball 2002
W. Ball, Rome in the East: The Transformation of an Empire (New York 2002).

Benjamin 1891
S. G. W. Benjamin, The Story of The Nations. Persia (New York 1891).

Boak 1921
A. E. R. Boak, A History of Rome to 565 AD (New York 1921).

Bournoutian 2006
G.A. Bournoutian, A Concise History of Armenian People (USA 2006).

Burney – Lang 1971
C. Burney – D. Lang, The Peoples of the Hills (London 1971).

Campbell 1993
B. Campbell, War and Diplomacy: Rome and Parthia, 31 BC–235 AD, in: J. Rich – G. Shipley (eds.), War and Society in Roman World (London 1993) 213–241.

Casson 2002
L. Casson, Antik Çağda Denizcilik ve Gemiler (İstanbul 2002).

Chahin 1987
M. Chahin, The Kingdom of Armenia (London 1987).

Champlin 2003
E. Champlin, Nero (London 2003).

Çiğdem 2011
S. Çiğdem, Roma-Parth İlişkilerinde Elegeia/Erzurum ve Çevresi, Atatürk Üniversitesi Sosyal Bilimler Dergisi 11/46, 2011, 97–118.

Colledge 1967
M. A. R. Colledge, The Parthians (London 1967).

Cook 1962
J. M. Cook, The Greeks in Ionia and the East, Ancient Peoples and Places 31 (London 1962).

Debevoise 1968
N. C. Debevoise, A Political History of Parthia (New York 1968).

Demir 2014
M. Demir, Roma-Armenia İlişkileri (MÖ 95 – MS 118), in: M. M. Hülagu et al. (eds.), Tarihte Türkler ve Ermeniler I (Ankara 2014) 55–97.

Frank 2004
T. Frank, An Economic History of Roma (Lancaster 2004).

Frankopan 2015
P. Frankopan, The Silk Roads: A New History of the World (Bloomsbury 2015).
Frye 1984
R.N. Frye, The History of Ancient Iran (Munich 1984).
Garsonian 1997
N. Garsonian, The Arsakuni Dynasty, in: R. G. Hovannisian (ed.), The Armenian People from Ancient to Modern Times I. The Dynastic Periods: From Antiquity to the Fourteenth Century (New York 1997) 63–94.
Gibbon 1987
E. Gibbon 1987, Roma İmparatorluğu'nun Gerileyiş ve Çöküş Tarihi 1–3, Trans.: A. Baltacıgil (İstanbul 1987).
Gruen 1996
E. S. Gruen, The Expansion of the Empire under Octavianus, in: A. K. Bowman – E. Champlin – A. Lintott (eds.), The Cambridge Ancient History X: The Augustan Empire, 43 BC–AD 69 [2](Cambridge 1996) 147–197.
Hammond 1996
N. G. L. Hammond, Alexander and Armenia, Phoenix 50, 1996, 130–137.
Hermann 1935
A. Hermann, Historical and Commercial Atlas of China (Massachussets 1935).
Jones 1971
A. H. M. Jones, The Cities of the Eastern Roman Provinces (Oxford 1971).
Jones 1998
A. H. M. Jones, Cities of the Eastern Roman Provinces (New York 1998).
Kaya 2004
M. A. Kaya, Romalılar, Parthlar ve Armenia Krallığı (İ.Ö. 92-İ.S. 4), Tarih İncelemeleri Dergisi 19/1, 2004, 73–86.
Kaya 1998
M. A. Kaya, Anadolu'da Roma Egemenliği ve Pompeius'un Siyasal Düzenlemeleri, Tarih İncelemeleri Dergisi 13, 1998, 163–173.
Keaveney 1991
A. Keaveney, Roman Treaties with Parthia circa 95–circa 64 B.C, AJPh 102/2, 1981, 195–212.
Keaveney 1992
A. Keaveney, Lucullus. A Life (London 1992).
Kurkjian 1964
V. M. Kurkjian, A History of Armenia (Dearborn 1964).
Litvinsky 1996
B. A. Litvinsky (ed.), The Crossroads of Civilizations: A.D. 250 to 750, HCCA 3 (Paris 1996).
Liu 2010
X. Liu 2010, The Silk Road in World History (New York 2010).
Mamandian 1965
H. Mamandian, The Trade and Cities of Armeniain Relation to Ancient World Trade (Lisbon 1965).

Manning 2014

J. G. Manning, At the Limits: Long-Distance Trade in the Time of Alexander the Great and Hellenistic Kings, in: V. H. Mair – J. Hickman (eds.), Reconfiguring the Silk Road: New Research on East-West Exchange in Antiquity (Philadelphia 2014) 5–14.

Martin 2013

T. R. Martin, Ancient Greece from Prehistoric to Hellenistic Times (London 2013).

Mayor 2013

A. Mayor, Mihtridates (İstanbul 2013).

Mommsen 2005

T. Mommsen, A History of Rome Under the Emperors 3(New York 2005).

Panossian 2006

R. Panossian, From Kings and Priests to Merchants and Commissars (Columbia 2006).

Payaslian 2007

S. Payaslian, The History of Armenia (USA 2007).

Redgate 1998

A. E. Redgate, The Armenians (Oxford 1998).

Richthofen 1877

F. V. Richthofen, Über die zenrtalasiatischen Seidenstrassen bis zum 2. Jahrhundert, Verhandlungen der Gesellschaft für Erdkunde,1877, 96–122.

Rostovtzeff 1936

M. I. Rostovtzeff, The Hellenistic World and Its Economic Development, The American Historical Review 41, 1936, 231–252.

Schmitt 1987

Armenia and Iran 2 (1987) 417 f. s. v. Armina. Achaemenid Province (R. Schmitt).

Sherwin-White 1977

A. N. Sherwin-White, Roman Involvement in Anatolia, 167–88 B.C., JRS 67, 1977, 62–75.

Sherwin-White 1983

A. N. Sherwin-White, Roman Foreign Policy in the East: 168 BC–AD 1 (Oklahoma 1983).

Shotter 2005

D. Shotter, Nero (London 2005).

Strootman 2011

R. Strootman, Hellenistic Court Society: The Seleukid Imperial Court Under Antiochos the Great, 223–187 BCE, in: J. Duindam – T. Artan – M. Kunt, Royal Courts in Dynastic States and Empires (Leiden 2011) 63–89.

Sullivan 1990

R. D. Sullivan, Near Eastern Royalty and Rome. 100–30 BC (Toronto 1990).

Swan 2004

P. M. Swan, The Augustan Succesion: An Historical Commentary on Cassius Dio's Roman History, Books 55–56 (9 B.C. – A.D. 14) (Oxford 2004).

Taylor 1936

L. R. Taylor, M. Titius and the Syrian Command, JRS 26/2, 1936, 161–173.

Tekin 2007
O. Tekin, Eski Anadolu ve Trakya (İstanbul 2007).

Tekin 2007
O. Tekin, Eski Yunan ve Roma Tarihine Giriş (İstanbul 2007).

Tezcan 2005
M. Tezcan, Eskiçağ'da Roma İmparatorluğu'nun Karadeniz Bölgesi Vasıtasıyla Hindistan ve Çin ile Ticareti, Başlangıçtan 20. yüzyıla Karadeniz Tarihi Sempozyumu I, 3–29.

Tezcan 2014
M. Tezcan, İran Armeniası (Pers Armenia), Tarihte Türkler ve Ermeniler (Ankara 2014) 149–182.

Thorley 1971
J. Thorley, The Silk Trade between China and the Roman Empire at Its Height, 'Circa' A.D. 90–130, Greece & Rome 18/1, 1971, 71–80.

Warmington 1974
E. H. Warmington, The Commerce Between the Roman Empire and India (Delhi 1974).

Yavuz 2014
M. F. Yavuz, Antikçağda Armenia: Kısa Bir Tarih, Yeni Türkiye 60, 2014, 1–12.

Yıldırım 2016
E. Yıldırım, Antik Yazarların Eserlerinde Sophene Bölgesi İle İlgili Anlatımlar, Gazi Üniversitesi Sosyal Bilimler Dergisi 3/7, 2016, 51–73.

Yorke 1896
V. W. Yorke, A Journey in the Valley of the Upper Euphrates, The Geographical Journal 8, 1896, 453–472.

Economic Mobility of Eastern Anatolia in the Byzantine Period

Ahmet Cuneydi Has

The Byzantine Empire, whose capital was the city of Constantinople (fig. 1) during the Middle Ages, dominated the three continents, Asia, Europe and Africa, geographically the most important strategic regions of the world from its foundation to its collapse.[1] Since the time of Emperor Justinian I,[2] the borders of the country, which has been expanding since the time of the Middle Ages, has gained enemies in every period (fig. 2). From Antalya to the south, to Egypt, to the Caucasus and Armenia to the east, to the south to southern Italy and Spain, which was reached during the reign of Basileios (fig. 3).[3] Although the borders have expanded to the Tigris Valley in the east of Anatolia, they have never been fixed.[4]

It entered a period of rapid pause with the Imperial dynasty of the Komnenos. Only the northwest of Anatolia, Thrace, part of Macedonia and the Straits remained of the Eastern Roman Empire. The Empire was erased from the stage of history by the conquest of Constantinople by the Ottoman Empire in the middle of the 15th century.

Economy

One of the two major sources of the economic system of the Byzantine Empire was the Roman Empire and the other one was Anatolia. The Anatolian peninsula was a transit trade zone that connects Asia to Europe and consists of regions with natural resources and different climates. In this respect, the Byzantine Empire was located in the region where the Silk and Spice roads reached the Mediterranean by connecting east-west economies. The state has advantageously used this position and has managed to have a say in world trade in every period. Even when the government's control over the economy loosened, private enterprises came to the forefront.

Important commercial points around Anatolia during the Byzantine Empire are: from land, in Tabriz in Iran, in Baghdad in Iraq, in Damascus in Syria; from the sea, there were Alexandria in Egypt, the island of Cyprus in the Mediterranean, Crimea in the north of the Black Sea, and the ports of Sinop, Samsun and Trabzon. These main points were connected by three main routes. The first one is the east-west route, the second is the north-south route, and the third is the diagonal route that connects the southeast with Istanbul. While the loss of Italy, the Balkans and Armenia in the periods of the disintegration of the Empire did not affect it economically, the weakening of trade with Syria, Egypt and Africa for political reasons seriously damaged the economy of the Byzantine Empire.[5]

Fig. 1: Constantinople City.

Themas (fig. 5),[6] which was estimated to have emerged during the period of I. Justinian (527–565 AD), when it was first established, expressed the provinces where the armies were established, but later assumed the role of controlling the economic and political administration.[7] These commanders were workers at the time of war and peasants in peacetime. Sivil Strategos "was a semi-civilian governor. In this context, the val Limitanei ra (Border governor), which was placed in the Roman border regions of the Themas, was similar to the military system of the land.[8]

The security of the Byzantine Empire and the dominance of the small regions provided the opportunity to recognize the dominance of small states.[9] The conquests changed the region's strategic and political geography, and the outpost and garrison system

Fig. 2: The History of the Empire.

Fig. 3: II. Basileios Age (976–1025).

(border guard) were monitored along the eastern border. Herakleios' Armeniakon covers the region of Armeniak, eastern Anatolia. The Armeniakon command occupied

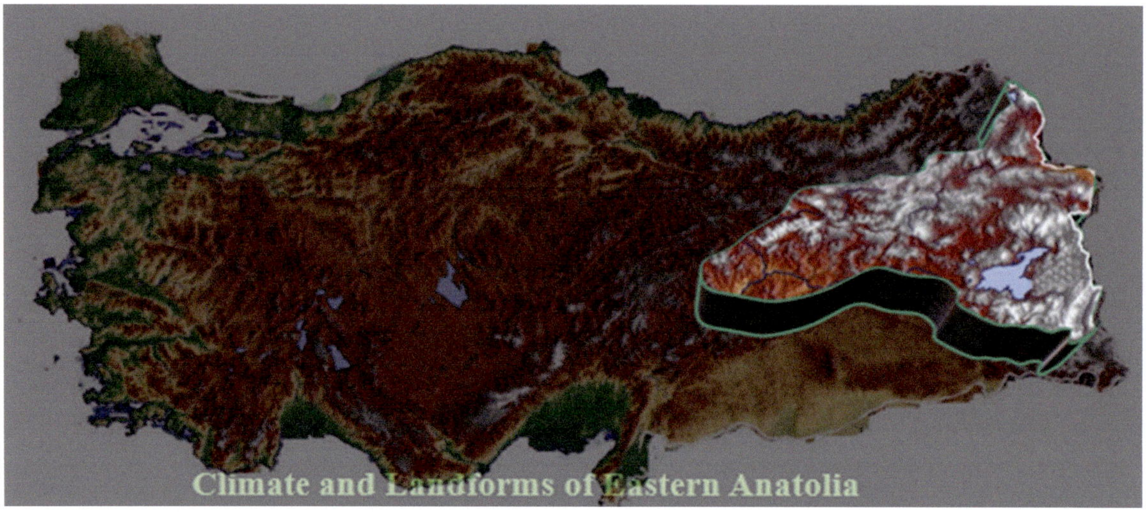

Fig. 4: Climate and Landforms os Eastern Anatolia.

the eastern and northern regions of Anatolia.[10] In fact, the region has generally placed its commercial role as a buffer zone and its military role in the military – administrative aspect.[11] This administrative system, which emphasized the political importance of the Eastern Anatolia Region in particular, was to provide control. In addition to the ongoing economic links between the east and the west, these traces were also important in the transition to the Holy Land.[12]

The Byzantine Empire in the Mediterranean, Aegean and Marmara regions, which are in the west of Anatolia and on the seaside, economy is generally active. He was able to maintain his sovereignty in the political and military spheres. This feature of the Eastern Anatolia Region due to difficult climate and ground shapes could not use enough. The fact that Sasanis and the Arabs started to be influential in the region was the most important factor in this, it became a transit area and fell into a passive situation.[13] But the political problems and conflicts between the Byzantine Empire and Arab thread did not enitrely complete the existing trade. Struggle with Sasanis, in particular, forced the Byzantine trade between Asia and Europe from the north of Eastern Anatolia to different commercial links with the Göktürks and the Khazars in Central Asia.

Using the Byzantine political and military power, it pursued the policy of maintaining all commercial products in its own geography. He tried to achieve this by using his strategic position effectively in every period. Starting from the end of the 7th century, all European trade was passing through Constantinople, a capital port that fulfilled its duty as a transit port and terminal.[14] The capital was Europe's richest and largest city from the 7th century to the 13th century.[15] The Eastern Anatolia Region has always assumed the same role as the highway in this period and after.

Although it was not as influential as Rome, it used commercial means and chose to collect more taxes. This tax collection system was based on the right to work in the right direction of the soil and labor, although it was not successful in later and was carried

Fig. 5: Development of the Byzantium Themes.

out in scattered ways.[16] The most important factor was the loss of land under the control of the Byzantine Empire.[17]

The geography of the Eastern Anatolia Region has not always shown itself in the same way everywhere, and has created differences in the forms of land, climate, vegetation, variety and quantity of production (fig. 4). However, these products were mainly produced by agriculture and animal husbandry, reflecting the characteristics of the region. Special craft branches such as forging, leatherwork and carpentry, which are specialized in rural areas of the region, are also seen. In this period, the mining industry was at the forefront of the Anatolian economy but we learned from the Armenian and Arabian sources that it was not used as effectively as the Romans'. In spite of this, the commercial policy of the Roman world has not been completely eradicated, but it has contributed to the trade.[18]

The hinterland of the agricultural economy along the Tigris and Euphrates rivers was filled with mountain and lowland settlements and had strategic importance.[19] Towards the end of the 4th century, Armenia was shared between the Byzantine Empire and the Sassanids (Persians). Karin (Erzurum), Erez (Erzincan) and Elazığ were included in the Byzantine Empire.[20] But the empire was not only in conflict with the Sassanid and Arabs in the east, but also with the Avars in the west, and it affected Eastern Anatolia,[21] both economically and politically.

In the beginning of Byzantine history, rare luxury items were mostly imported from the east, jewelery from India and Iran, and silk from China.[22] Such luxury goods were state monopoly, especially the workshops where they were working close to the center where both men and women worked.

Although the most important commercial products of the empire were grain and silk, the number of goods traded in Istanbul and other provinces of the empire was quite high. The most important ones are olive oil, wine, salty fish, meat, vegetables, salt, timber, carpet, wax, ceramic, wood and linen.[23] In addition, luxury items such as perfumes and spices, as well as slave trade was intense. Mine, ceramic, textile, glass, silk, ivory, gold and silver works were evaluated as a secondary production to manufacturing and craftsman.

This region has been an important transit point between the east and west of the commercial goods during the Byzantine Empire period, as in every period. It has played an important role in supplying products from the far east and the east to the capital Constantinople. The role of the soil and the harsh climate have been important in assuming this role. But the struggles that took place with the Sassanids and the Arabs from time to time caused negative results in the region as well as economically. The Eastern Anatolia Region, which is close to the disintegration phase of the Empire, has emerged from the sovereignty of the state and lost its importance.

It is to better understand and evaluate the commercial life of the Byzantine Anatolian Caucasus and the Islamic world in the east; the south coast, the Aegean Islands and the Greek world with Constantinople.

Notes

[1] This subject has been discussed more comprehensively in Turkish in L.G. Gökçek – E. Yildirim – O. Pekşen, Economic and Agricultural Life in the Ancient Ages of the Anatolia (Istanbul 2018) 459–544. – Bayness – Moss 1953, 63.

[2] Evans 1970, 218–223 .

[3] Ostragorsky 1986, 292; Lemerle 1965, 95.

[4] Decker 2007, 221.

[5] Treadgold 1997, 402.

[6] Güçlüay 2013, 161.

[7] Rosser 1984, 383.

[8] Decker 2007, 217; Haldon 2005, 117; Gregory 2005, 362.

[9] Honıgmann 1970, 145.

[10] Haldon 2005, 117; Lemerle 1965, 77.

[11] Bamyacı – Güçlüay 2018, 284.

[12] Bamyacı – Güçlüay 2018, 284.

[13] Decker 2007, 217; Lemerle 1965, 95; Vasiliev 1962, 303.

[14] Bayness – Moss 1953, 70.

[15] Harrison 1900, 13.

[16] Haldon 2005, 126.

[17] Bamyacı – Güçlüay 2018, 284.
[18] Laiou 2002, 1133.
[19] Gregory 2005, 84.
[20] Sağır 2014, 184.
[21] Bamyacı – Güçlüay 2018, 286.
[22] Lemerle 1965, 66.
[23] Bahar 2011, 182.

Image Credits

Fig. 1–2: <http://www.britannica.com/>. – Fig. 3: <http://www.quora.com/>. – Fig. 4: <https://tr.wikipedia.org/wiki/T%C3%BCrkiye_co%C4%9Frafyas%C4%B1>. – Fig.5: <http://www.hellenicaworld.com>.

References

Bahar 2011
H. Bahar, Roma ve Bizans Tarihi, Kömen Yayınları (Konya 2012).

Bamyacı – Güçlüay 2018
M. E. Bamyacı – S. Güçlüay, İmparator Herakleios Dönemi (610–641) Bizans İmparatorluğu'nun Genel Ekonomisi ve Ticaret Politikası, The Journal of International Social Sciences 8, 2018, 281–288.

Baynes-Boss 1953
N. H. Baynes – L. B. Boss, Byzantium an Introduction to East Roman Civilization (London 1953).

Decker 2007
M. Decker, Frontier Settlement and Economy in the Byzantine East, DOP 61, 2007, 217–267.

Evans 1970
J. A. S Evans, Justinian and the Historian Procopius, GaR 17, 1970, 218–223.

Gregory 2005
T. E. Gregory, A History of Byzantium (Oxford 2005).

Güçlüay 2013
S. Güçlüay, Bizans İmparatorluğunda Toprak Sistemi İçerisinde Themalar (IV–VII. Yüzyıllar), in: Fırat Üniversitesi Ortadoğu Araştırmaları Merkezi, Ortadoğu Araştırmaları Dergisi, Ocak, 2011 (Elazığ 2013) 63–89.

Haldon 2005
J. Haldon, The Palgrave Atlas of Byzantine History (London 2005).

Harrison 2007
F. Harrison, Byzantine History in the Early Middle Ages (Toronto 2007).

Honigman 1970
E. Honigman, Eastern Border of the Byzantine State (Istanbul 1970).

Laiou 2002
A. E. Laiou, The Economic History of Byzantium, Dumbarton Oaks Studies 39 (Washington 2002).
Lemerle 1965
P. Lemerle, Histoire de Byzance (Paris 1965).
Ostrogorsky 1986
G. Ostrogorsky, History of the Byzantine State (New Jersey 1986).
Rosser 2001
J. H. Rosser, Historical Dictionary of Byzantium (New Jersey 2001).
Sağır 2014
G. Sağır, Bizans İmparatorluğu Dönemi'nde Anadolu'da Ermeni Yerleşimleri, in: Metin Hülagü (ed.), Tarihte Türkler ve Ermeniler: İlkçağ ve Ortaçağ (Ankara 2014) 183–205.
Treadgold 1997
W. Treadgold, A History of the Byzantine State and Society (California 1997).
Vasiliev 1952
A. Vasiliev, History of the Byzantine Empire 324–1453 (Wisconsin 1952).

The Economic Structure of the Eastern Anatolian Highlands from the Urartian Period to the End of Late Antiquity – Panel Conclusion

Mehmet Işikli

The 19th International Congress of Classical Archaeology: "Archaeology and Economy in the Ancient World", with the panel entitled "The Economic Structure of the Eastern Anatolian Highlands from the Urartian Period to the End of Late Antiquity". We delivered five different presentations, which focus on the economic structure of the Eastern Anatolian Highlands within the scope of this panel. The economic structure was discussed in detail from the Paleolithic period to Late Antiquity through the instrument of these presentations. In each presentation the economic structure of the period will be studied and analyzed along with the archaeological and cultural background of the related period. In order of presentation, they are as follows:

- Ayşegül Akın ARAS, "Socio-economic Structure of the Eastern Anatolia Region before Urartian Kingdom"
- Mehmet IŞIKLI – Oğuz ARAS, "Observations on the Urartian Economy in Light of the Excavations at Ayanis Castle"
- Leila AFSHARI – Soraya AFSHARI, "The Economic condition of the Eastern Anatolian Highland (Armenia Satrapy) during the Achaemenid Period"
- Elif YAVUZ – Nusret Burak ÖZSOY, "The Economic and Political State of Eastern Anatolia during the Classical Period"
- Ahmet Cuneydi HAS, "Economic Mobility in Eastern Anatolia during the Byzantine Period"

Before the presentations, some general information was provided about regional geography and archaeology. As you know, the Eastern Anatolian Highland is part of the mountainous belt lying between the Taurus Mountains and the Great Caucasus Mountain range, which creates the northern border of the ancient Near East. The geography of Eastern Anatolia, which covers 163,000 km^2, is formalized by high plateaus, long mountain ranges with heights reaching to 3000 meters, and low, flat depression lines, which lie between the ranges. This high mountainous zone, known as the "Eastern Anatolian Highland", receives heavy rain and snow because of its altitude, and the water supply is very substantial. From this region rise the major rivers of the Near East: the Euphrates, Tigris, Kura and Araxes rivers, making this region the reservoir of the Mesopotamia and Caucasus world. This vast and varied region is comprised of four cultural and geographical sub-regions. These sub-regions (from north to south) are the Erzurum-Kars Plateau, the Van-Mus Region centered in the Van Lake Basin, the Upper Euphrates Valley connecting between the eastern highland and the northern Mesopotamian lowland, and the mountainous Hakkâri Region located in the southeastern corner of Eastern Anatolia.

As it is observed, this extraordinary region presents adverse aspects, both geographically and environmentally. However, from an archaeological viewpoint, the region is not well known. In addition to this, archaeological research, which has been ongoing for almost a century, can only enlighten us with the general outlines of regional archaeology. We have some knowledge of the prehistoric, late prehistoric and Iron and Classical ages of the region, but we need more details. Now we shall examine the economic structure of the highlands, when considering archaeological periods in the light of available evidence.

As it was demonstrated, our region of Eastern Anatolia is the most problematic sub-region of the ancient Near East in many aspects. The basis of this situation is concerned mostly with geographic and environmental difficulties. These negative conditions, which have arisen from the geographic-climatic situation, have always imposed a hard life on the people living in the hilly zones. The economic systems and structures of the people and culture were shaped according to these conditions within each period. Throughout the ages they had to resort to the main subsistence strategies like animal husbandry and limited agricultural activities. On the other hand, there were some important reasons for staying here: its specific location, and its richness in raw materials. This harsh region has always been on the periphery of, and/or exploited by, imperial powers and great empires. Because of its special location, the region has always been crucial to these powers because of the main routes passing through it, and their control of the hilly zone, by way of borders and road security, was always very important.

Now, the results obtained within our presentations and the periods should be considered and discussed. Firstly, we shall focus on the pre-Urartian Periods, namely from the prehistoric ages up to the formation of the Urartian State. These prehistoric ages, including the Paleolithic and Neolithic periods of the highlands, are the least known periods in terms of archaeology. The Eastern Anatolian Highland has wealthy sources of obsidian, which was a strategic raw material of the prehistoric period, and for this reason the region was unique for prehistoric societies living in neighboring lands. Recently, some projects have shown that an interregional trade network was dependent on the obsidian of the region. The other data group related to this subject is rock art, which can be found in many places in the mountainous zone. Unfortunately, the relevant experts did not systematically study these drawings on the rock facades. According to some scholars these drawings on the rocks, along with some distinct survey materials, were the traces of hunter and gathering groups who were living on the lowlands of northern Mesopotamia during the Upper Paleolithic to Pre-pottery Neolithic periods, and who moved across the highlands for hunting and collecting raw materials.

From the late Neolithic period and during the Chalcolithic period, this sub-region was a target area for the great (and strong) Mesopotamian cultures, such as Halaf, Ubaid and Uruk. The sub-region is one of the significant expansion areas of these imperialist cultural structures. This region is rich in raw materials, always essential for Mesopotamia, which is poor in raw resources. The hilly northern part of the highland had some relationships with the southern Caucasus during the Late Chalcolithic period. As it was shown, beginning from the Chalcolithic period there were two different cultural zones in the highlands: the southern section, which integrated and faced towards the Mesopotamian world, and the northern section, which was more localized and had relationships with the southern Caucasus.

During the long transition period from the Late Chalcolithic to Early Bronze Age I, a cultural phenomenon, which we call the Kura-Araxes Culture, expanded right across the hilly zone. The semi-nomads and settled societies of this cultural phenomenon survived on a subsistence strategy based on agriculture and animal husbandry. The Upper Euphrates Valley, which was the heartland of a dynamic north-south commercial network, was a center of attraction for these pastoral groups. Towards the end of the Early Bronze Age, new groups from the north, known as the "Kurgan People", entered into the hilly zone. The societies of this period were mostly moving pastoral groups, and stockbreeding was still the dominant subsistence strategy. Agricultural activities were scarce. From the late Bronze Age to the beginning of the Early Iron Age, the chiefdoms, from which the Urartian State was created, appeared in the hilly zone. This process is known as "Early State Formation" and "Early Socio-Political Complexes" by some scholars.

The Urartian State, which was created in the middle of the 9th century BCE, was the first central political unit of the hilly zone, and it was during this process that the hilly zone met with the literary traditions and state formation ideas of Mesopotamia. Accordingly, the economy of the highland became institutionalized. The economy was recorded and controlled by political (royal) and religious (temple) powers; however, we do not know the particular roles and activities, which were undertaken. The Urartian economy covered a large domain, which varied from agricultural activities to spoils of war. It is possible to observe some of the details concerning this institutionalized economic system with the help of written documentations such as inscriptions and bullae. One rich Urartian site in terms of written sources is Ayanis Castle, which dates to the 7th century BCE. The excavations at Ayanis castle have presented us with very rich data including written sources and architectural remains relating to the Urartian economy; however, the Urartian records concerning the economic system are very limited. For this reason we do not know its details, and there are many essential problems related to this subject which remain unsolved.

After the collapse of the Urartian Kingdom at the beginning of 6th century BCE, the hilly zone was left unconstrained for a brief period in terms of political control. After a short time this political gap would be filled by the Achaemenid Empire, which was the new superpower of the ancient Near East. The hilly zone was a part of the Armenian Satrapy of the Achaemenid Empire for almost 200 years. Unfortunately, it is not easy to follow the archaeological traces of the Achaemenid Kingdom in the hilly zone, or even Anatolia overall. Our knowledge about the social, political, and economic conditions of the region during this process is very limited. According to some written evidence from the Persian and Classical periods, the Armenian Satrapy had an important position in the economy of the Achaemenid Empire by way of raw materials such as ores, and by trade routes. Unfortunately, we know very few things concerning the dynamics of the economic structure/system in the Highlands during the Achaemenid period.

The unclear and blurred picture, which we have relating to the socio-economic structure of the Eastern Anatolian Highlands was to continue in this way following the Classical and Late Antiquity periods, including the Hellenistic, Roman and Byzantine periods. The archaeological traces of Hellenistic, Roman and Byzantine Empires are very scanty in the hilly zone, although the situation for Byzantium is a bit better. The relationships of the great exploitation empires like Greece and Rome within the highlands were based largely on the supply of those necessary raw materials, which we have mentioned, and on roads and border security. Actually this type of harsh, rugged and rural area with its economy based on agriculture and animal husbandry is not of vital importance to these large-scale economic systems. To control and improve this kind of formidable geography requires a huge budget. Most of the imperialist political powers kept away from attempting these improvements, and they just prefer to exploit them. The hilly zone, including the Eastern Anatolian Highland, has continued to follow its subsistence existence and similar destiny during Classical and Late Antiquity periods. This marginal zone of the ancient Near East has appeared on the periphery of the great empires time after time because of its extraordinary geography, its wealth of raw materials and its special location in dominating trade routes through the ages – a position, which its resilient and tough peoples have never been prepared to sacrifice to outsiders.

Printing and Binding
Books on Demand GmbH
In de Tarpen 42, 22848 Norderstedt, Germany